JEROME ROBBINS

Jerome Robbins

A Life in Dance

—◆◆◆—

WENDY LESSER

Yale

UNIVERSITY
PRESS

New Haven and London

Yale University Press books may be purchased in quantity for educational,
business, or promotional use. For information, please e-mail sales.press@yale.edu
(U.S. office) or sales@yaleup.co.uk (U.K. office).

Set in Janson Oldstyle type by Integrated Publishing Solutions,
Grand Rapids, Michigan.
Printed in the United States of America.

Library of Congress Control Number: 2017964064
ISBN 978-0-300-19759-4 (hardcover : alk. paper)

A catalogue record for this book is available from the British Library.

This paper meets the requirements of ANSI/NISO Z39.48-1992
(Permanence of Paper).

10 9 8 7 6 5 4 3 2 1

Frontispiece: *Jerome Robbins*, New York, 1948
© The Irving Penn Foundation

For Richard

It was my homosexuality I was afraid would be exposed I thought. It was my once having been a Communist that I was afraid would be exposed. None of these. I was & have been—& still have terrible pangs of terror when I feel that my career, work, veneer of accomplishments would be taken away (by HUAC, or by critics) that I panicked & crumbled & returned to that primitive state of terror—the facade of Jerry Robbins would be cracked open, and behind everyone would finally see Jerome Wilson Rabinowitz.

—notebook entry from 1976

CONTENTS

---◆◆◆---

Overture

HE MAY WELL have been the most hated man on Broad-way. "Mean as a snake," said Helen Gallagher, a performer who worked with him on several shows, and her words echoed the abundant testimony of others. A few dancers loved him deeply, and many more admired him, but almost all of them feared him. In particular, they feared the vicious outbursts that would tear them down to nothing, reducing them to a humiliating puddle of tears and sweat. He felt he had to break everything down in order to build it up in a better form. The performers understood that. But it was hard if you were the material being shaped.

A much-repeated story from one of his Broadway shows (probably *Billion Dollar Baby*, though it's been attributed to several others) points to the intensity of the collective resentment. During one rehearsal, Robbins was addressing the dancers and

I

singers as they stood on the stage of the theater. He had his back to the orchestra and the rest of the auditorium, and the performers were ranged around him, facing him. As he spoke, he stepped backward. Then he stepped backward again, dangerously close to the edge of the stage. Nobody said a word. He took another step back and fell into the pit, and not one of them came to his aid. Their silence, in the close-knit world of stage performers, was tantamount to a village stoning.

If you had asked Jerome Robbins why he acted the way he did, he would have said it was all in service of the art. And for the most part it was. When he told the dancers playing Puerto Ricans and whites that they could not associate with members of the opposite gang during the entire rehearsal period for *West Side Story*—and when, to exacerbate tensions between the two groups, he circulated scurrilous gossip about Jets among Sharks and about Sharks among Jets—he did so in order to create the level of manifest hatred that he felt the show demanded. Similarly, when he jointly auditioned the two actors who eventually got the central roles of Maria and Tony, he first called them onto the stage separately. To Carol Lawrence, he said, "I want you to get lost on the stage somewhere, so he can't see you. I'm going to bring him in and let him do 'Maria.' After that, if he can find you, do the balcony scene. If he *can't* find you, you don't have an audition." Once she had hidden herself on a grating fifteen feet above the stage, he brought in Larry Kert and told him the same thing. The poor guy sang his heartfelt song, meanwhile frantically glancing around the stage and not finding his Maria anywhere. Just as he was about to give up, his co-star hissed, "Tony!" and he turned, saw her, and clambered up the rickety ladder to her side, where they finished the scene in an overflowing spirit of intimate relief. Leonard Bernstein— who, as the composer, had been privy to this scene—walked from his seat in the audience down to the front of the stage and said, "That is the most mesmerizing audition I've ever seen in my life."

Rehearsals were nightmarish experiences, with everyone exhausted by the long days, forced to go through ten or twenty versions of a single scene as Robbins worked out what he wanted. Recalling her role in the ballet *Age of Anxiety*, Tanaquil Le Clercq complained that Robbins "rehearsed it to death . . . he changed it all the time," working her and the other dancers until they were all "goofy with fatigue." The choreographer thought nothing of exposing his performers to physical pain, as when he made one of his gang members lie on the blisteringly hot New York City pavement during the filming of *West Side Story*: "Where do you think you're going?" Robbins snarled at the dancer when he tried to get up between takes. At other times he would freely ladle out insults, along the lines of "I thought you were a better dancer than that."

And he was no kinder to his actors. When, during the out-of-town tryouts for *Fiddler on the Roof*, he gave notes to Austin Pendleton about his role as the son-in-law Motel, he sneered at this once-favored protégé, "I don't know what's happened to you. I had to walk out during the wedding scene last night because the idea of that girl being forced to marry you was so revolting. You've lost that tenacity—you're not worth her time." Years later, reflecting back on this moment, Pendleton admitted that Robbins "was seeing a weakness in me he had never seen, a complacency, a limpness. It was cruel but it addressed exactly what had to happen between me and the role. He was right." And Robbins's own comments about his cruelty contained much the same defense: "I blow, but it only happens when the person isn't doing the job I think they should and not giving back as much as I'm putting into it."

What he was putting in was his whole self, along with everything he knew about the world and its people and the emotions that governed their lives. That was the novelty of Jerome Robbins's idea of performance, whether it was a Broadway show or a ballet for one of New York's well-regarded dance companies. They were not just entertainments, in Robbins's mind; they were not just finely wrought products of a traditional art form (though they were both those things as well). Those patently artificial forms—the American musical, the court-derived ballet —were for him the expressions of a felt reality, and if the actors and dancers putting them on could not feel them as real, then the artworks would be worth nothing in the end. "I emerged a different person" was how Austin Pendleton described his response to the last-minute critique of his Motel part, and that was what Robbins wanted every time: complete transformation. He wanted it of himself just as much as, and perhaps more than, he wanted it of everyone else. Observing that he was "just murder to work with," Trude Rittman, the rehearsal pianist for *Billion Dollar Baby*, said her complaint "was not that he did it to me, but he did it to the kids and he did it to himself. . . . This man constantly murdered himself. He was so high-strung and tormented."

It should come as no surprise that the man who envisioned a parent-less utopia in *Peter Pan*, and who created one of the great stage monster-mothers in *Gypsy*, came from a routinely dysfunctional family. The remark made by the psychoanalyst Adam Phillips—"They used to call it family life; now they call it child abuse"—could have been designed to convey Jerome Robbins's early life.

Jerome Wilson Rabinowitz was born in New York City on October 11, 1918, to Harry and Lena Rabinowitz, who shortly thereafter moved to New Jersey. Their son was given all the cultural advantages favored by upwardly mobile immigrant Jews. He took piano lessons and even performed in public recitals, garnering a positive review in the local paper at the age of six. When he expressed interest in his older sister Sonia's dance classes, he was allowed to attend those too. A gifted and precocious writer, he did well in English and history at school, and he was also a skilled amateur artist. He earned plenty of warm praise and good grades over the years, including an A+ for a high-school essay called "My Selves," in which he said: "I stand before a mirror. Ahead, two dark eyes are looking back at me beneath a shock of black hair. . . . Slowly the mask begins to rise, revealing another face." The masks all have the same features but vastly different expressions, and there are many of them. "Faster and faster they come, spreading over the mirror, the walls, the room, the earth. They all look at me with blank vacant eyes where, if they were over my face, my eyes would show through. They are all me, every one."

This eternally self-scrutinizing boy was an odd creature to emerge from the lower-middle-class environs of Weehawken, New Jersey. According to both his and his sister's memories, the Rabinowitz household essentially revolved around parental concerns—most notably the family business, the Comfort Corset Company, which was run by their self-engrossed, rarely affectionate father with the active assistance of their forceful mother. Lena was also responsible for a range of volunteer activities as well as family matters involving her large group of sisters, among whom she was the acknowledged head. Still, she did take time out of her busy schedule to drive her children to lessons and performances, even those that took place across the river in New York.

As a small boy, Jerry was markedly devoted to his mother, constantly seeking her approval and often failing to get it. When he made her angry, for instance, Lena would pick up the phone and fake a call: "Hello, is this the orphanage? Come and get my boy. I don't want him any more." He would cry and plead for her forgiveness. Once he even wrote her a profoundly creepy yet typically intelligent note of apology:

> Dear Mommy ·
>   Im very SORRY
>   and so
> S is for sacrifice that you do for me
> O is for oweing which I owe to thee
> R is for rude which Im sometimes to you
> R is for apology Im trying to do
> Y is for you dear, this poem's at its end
>   your my sweetheart my lover
>   and your my best friend
>   Jerry

One presumes this performance accomplished its mission, since Lena proudly saved it among her son's childhood papers— although she also crossed out some of the words, icily correct- ing them with her own suggestions. Clearly Robbins came by his cruel perfectionism honestly.

By the time Jerry graduated from high school, his sister, who was six years older, was already at work in New York, sup- porting herself as a salesgirl at Macy's and as a model for the artist Reginald Marsh while also performing in weekend dance productions under the name Sonya Robyns. Harry and Lena wanted their son to go to work as well, preferably for the Com- fort Corset Company, but he resisted, and so he was permit- ted to attend New York University for a year. By the end of his freshman year, though, he was failing two out of his five courses, and Harry, whose income had declined as the Depres- sion deepened, insisted his son drop out and come to work at the corset factory. This experiment floundered within a few months—Jerry, although still unsure which paths he wanted to pursue in life, was convinced that "running the Comfort Cor- set Co. was not among them"—at which point the eighteen-year-old boy made a deal with his parents: they would give him room and board and the daily ferry fare to New York for a year, and he would see what he could make of himself. At the end of that time, it would be the factory or nothing.

It was Sonia who helped Jerry get his first foothold in New York, introducing him in the fall of 1936 to Gluck Sandor, the man who, with his wife, ran the Dance Center group with which she had been performing. Jerry had only taken a few dance lessons at this point—with a Martha Graham acolyte in Greenwich Village and then with Alys Bentley, Sonia's Isadora Duncan–style teacher—but he had perfect pitch and an excellent sense of rhythm, could move naturally and expressively, and had won acclaim performing in a series of vaudeville-like routines and Gilbert & Sullivan operettas at Kittatinny, their extended family's summer camp in the Poconos. Sandor had Jerry do a few improvisations on command (one of them as the god Shiva, whom Jerry had never heard of before) and then hired him on the spot. Having changed his own name from Sammy Gluck to make it sound less Jewish and more stage-worthy, Sandor encouraged Jerome Rabinowitz to do the same, and by February of 1937, when the Dance Center presented a WPA-funded concert at the Federal Music Project's theater on Fifty-Fourth Street, "Gerald Robbins" was listed among the dancers. After a short period in which the order and spelling shifted several times, the name hardened permanently into Jerome Robbins. By the fall of 1937 both Sonia and Jerry were on Sandor's regular payroll, thus banishing forever the prospect of the corset factory and setting Robbins on his destined path.

Choreography entered the picture early—Robbins enrolled in Bessie Schönberg's composition class near Union Square— and so did ballet. Sandor urged Robbins to take those lessons as soon as he hired him: "You better study ballet," Sandor said, "because it's going to come back. You should get that technique

7

on your body while you still can, while you're still growing." Jerry resisted the idea at first, viewing ballet as "stodgy and awful" in comparison to modern dance: "I had only danced in bare feet and full of freedom to improvise as I 'felt' it to music. Ballet had nothing to do with dancing." But then, having been given a free ticket to the Ballet Russes at the Metropolitan Opera House, he saw an electrifying performance by Alexandra Danilova in a ballet by Massine, and that permanently won him over to the beauty of the form. He first took ballet classes with a free WPA teacher and then, when he became more serious about it, moved over to Ella Daganova. (That was after he tried, without success, to enroll in the new School of American Ballet, recently opened by the émigré George Balanchine.) Daganova, an American who had given herself a Russian name to attract students, let Robbins take up to two barre classes a day in return for his janitorial work at her studio. And at the same time as he was absorbing all these lessons and performing with the Dance Center, Jerry also, with Sandor's help, began taking on small roles at the Yiddish Art Theatre, so he was developing his acting skills even as he was working on movement.

But Robbins's real education came during the summers, when—like many dancers, singers, and actors, from Danny Kaye and Imogene Coca to members of the Ballet Theatre and Martha Graham dance troupes—he moved to Camp Tamiment, a Catskills-like resort that happened to be located in the Poconos, not far from his family's camp. In those pre-air-conditioning days, New York City emptied out as the performing groups all went on hiatus, and their temporarily unemployed members took on the kind of work that was available in vacation resorts. Every week of the summer, these talented performers put on a different Broadway-level revue, complete with dancing, singing, acting, and even lighting and sets. Tamiment was "my first contact with other professional theatre people," according to Robbins, and he took to the collaborative efforts with energy and delight. During the four summers he spent there, he made his first real attempts at choreography: solos, duets, trios, and even "my first tries at sketches of little ballets." But even beyond the dance and performance experience, he was learning something about the essence of theatricality, and it was the comedians who really taught him this. "I was as attentive a fan as if I were her understudy," he said of Imogene Coca, with whom he worked on several sketches. "I was thrilled to watch the simpleness and clarity of her mind. Her acting was connected and personal, her taste and sensitivity were almost painfully touching. I believe I learned more from her about timing and humor than anyone else."

Not every dance or Broadway show that Jerome Robbins went on to make in his lifetime was humorous in nature. On the contrary, many of them were deadly serious, and even the comic productions had their dark elements. But something about the nature of comedy—the way it promises something and then delivers on that promise; its collaborative relationship with an audience, whom it exists to both unsettle and delight; its pleasure in the gemlike structure of a joke, which needs to be constructed and executed perfectly if it is to work at all; above all, perhaps, its understanding of the highly expressive and potentially wordless capacities of the human body—underlies every great work that Robbins created. Unlike many choreographers, he was essentially a narrative artist, yet unlike most other Broadway directors and producers, he also understood that the important meanings take place at a level beyond plot. These two things rarely go together, but in Robbins they meshed, and both of them are qualities he could have derived from his Tamiment summers. Those early exposures to comic genius may well be what enabled him to develop to such a high pitch his theatrical, narrative imagination.

Think for a moment about what such an imagination entails. The narrative artist (a category of which Robbins was perhaps one of the twentieth century's most powerful exemplars) is preoccupied with doling out his material in a particular order, to produce a varying but related set of emotions and realizations. Among his key implements are timing and sequencing, which in turn can be used to induce anticipation and suspense. By this means audience members become collaborators as well as recipients, for the narrative artwork resides, in large part, in the viewer's encounter with it: that is, a narrative must by definition exist in time, and only when the work is performed on a stage does that vital dynamic come into play. Moreover, it happens differently every time, with each new viewer and then with each repeated viewing, so that the narrative remains always open, never closed and finished.

Narrative, or drama, is not identical with story-telling. Music without words can have it, and so can dances without plots. It may take you longer to recognize narrative in an abstract or plotless work, but the tendency can still be there, resting in the twists and turns of the choreography, the rhythms and reversals of the music. We progress from walking to leaping to standing still: that can be the narrative. Or: we go away from the home key and then come back to it, with variations in between. The theatrical capacity resides not in the story being told, but in the creator's manner of telling it.

Narrative is not, of course, equivalent to meaning. In fact, a work that knows and announces its own meaning too clearly generally fails on the narrative level, because it retains no sense of open possibilities and therefore has nowhere to go: it is fixed and unyielding, whereas truly narrative works are filled with movement. (This is true even when they are still works, like paintings or sculptures. Think of Bernini's great marble pieces, like *Apollo and Daphne* and *The Rape of Proserpina*, which are as fluid as snapshots taken from life.) Not that narrative artworks are meaningless—on the contrary, if they are any good they are replete with meaning, with multiple meanings. But a good narrative artwork does not tell you its meaning in a direct and translatable way, just as it does not convey to you in explicit form its creator's intentions. The creator must *have* intentions for the artwork to succeed, but they will never be identical to a viewer's experience of the artwork. That is part of the free play by which art becomes something more than even its creator can account for.

Granted, a narrative imagination carries certain dangers. It can lean in the direction of the sentimental or the overly melodramatic, sometimes even stepping over that line. It can be vulgar. It can turn simplicity into simple-mindedness. All of these problems are far less likely to occur in abstract art, where simplicity is almost always a virtue and sentimentality is practically impossible. But precisely because narrative art takes these risks—the way comedy does, too, by constantly confronting the possibility that its jokes will fall flat—the mode is capable of bringing us something that we can't necessarily get with more coolly formal works.

By the time his Tamiment summers were over, at the beginning of the 1940s, Jerome Robbins had not necessarily grasped any of this consciously. Perhaps he *never* grasped any of it consciously (though, as a lifelong psychoanalytic patient and a constant diary-keeper, he was probably more self-aware than most). But whether he knew it or not, those Tamiment revues, along with the performers he met while putting them on, provided him with exactly the kind of intuitive knowledge he would need to start on his real career.

Fancy Free

IT WAS NOT until 1943 that Jerome Robbins was given the opportunity to choreograph his first real ballet, and by that time he was already an integral part of the New York dance world.

During the late 1930s, while still living at home with his parents and commuting by ferry to New York, he had left Gluck Sandor's company and begun auditioning for Broadway musicals—an extremely discouraging experience, with its impersonal cattle calls and its repeated rejections, though he kept at it nonetheless. Eventually he got his break from, of all people, George Balanchine. Known in Europe as a ballet choreographer, the Russian-born Balanchine had divided his time since coming to America between classical ballet and the more demotic American form of musical comedy. His first attention-getting work was with Rodgers & Hart's 1936 show *On Your Toes*, for which he choreographed the ballet "Slaughter on Tenth Avenue." After that he was in great demand on Broadway (the critic John Martin thought he should make his career in musical comedy rather than ballet), and he had since done two more Rodgers & Hart musicals, *Babes in Arms* and *I Married an Angel*, as well as a Hollywood movie, *The Goldwyn Follies*.

Now, in 1938, he was casting for a Frederick Loewe musical called *The Great Lady*, and the skinny young kid from Weehawken caught his eye. "He picked me and I was very, very proud of that," Robbins recalled years later. "The dancers in the show were almost entirely from the School of American Ballet, which I didn't go to." Robbins was only a member of the chorus—a great corps de ballet, which also featured Alicia Alonso and Nora Kaye—but he felt that Balanchine singled him out for special "little things."

The Great Lady didn't last long, but Robbins soon found employment in another Broadway production, *The Straw Hat Revue*, which paid him a steady $40 a week (and for which he even did a bit of uncredited choreography). The income was so encouraging—and the family environment so discouraging—that Jerry took this opportunity to move out of the Rabinowitz house and into a small furnished room in Manhattan. After that show ended its run, he won a place in another Balanchine-choreographed production, *Keep Off the Grass*, which featured a roster of stars including Jimmy Durante, Ray Bolger, Jackie Gleason, the clown Emmett Kelly, and the dancer José Limón. This time, Balanchine thought so highly of Robbins's work that he made him the understudy for Limón. But the show lasted only five weeks, closing for good in June of 1940, and Robbins never got to perform the Limón role.

By this time, though, he had secured a job with the newly formed Ballet Theatre, an experimental enterprise that was largely bankrolled by Lucia Chase, a wealthy woman who was also an aspiring ballerina. The new company, which promised to present "The Greatest Ballets of All Time Staged by the Greatest Collaboration in Ballet History!," premiered in New York in January of 1940, and its first two-month season was a great success. Jerry had not been able to join at the beginning, since he was still engaged on *Keep Off the Grass*, but by wangling himself a late audition and persistently bombarding the company's manager, Richard Pleasant, with fervent pleas, he was able to obtain a signed contract for Ballet Theatre's 1940 summer season at $32.50 a week. The salary was of course useful, but the real benefit lay in the people he worked with—the choreographers Antony Tudor, Agnes de Mille, and Michel Fokine, and the dancers Nora Kaye, Muriel Bentley, John Kriza, Donald Saddler, and others, many of whom were to remain his friends and collaborators in the years that followed.

Ballet Theatre had its financial ups and downs, and Lucia Chase soon began to feel that even her large fortune would not cover all the ever-mounting bills. By 1941 she had signed over managerial control to Sol Hurok, who brought in an income by touring the company all over America, mainly with Russian-dance programming. In December of 1941, partway into the first Hurok season, Pearl Harbor was attacked and America entered the war, further exacerbating the troupe's economic problems, since in the face of that kind of universal cataclysm, who would want to be watching ballet? The war produced specific problems for the dancers as well—namely, the fear of being drafted. Jerome Robbins and a close friend with whom he was living at the time, the playwright Horton Foote, were both called up by their local draft board in the spring of 1942. Foote got a 4F disqualification because of a previously undiscovered hernia. Robbins, instead, relied on the interview. "Have you ever had a homosexual experience?" the examiner queried, to which Robbins honestly answered, "Yes." As a follow-up, the examiner asked him when the most recent such experience had occurred. "Last night," Jerry said.

For years, Robbins had understood that he was attracted to both men and women, and he had acted on both kinds of desire. His first homosexual encounter had taken place soon after he joined the Gluck Sandor company in New York. It's less easy to pin down his first heterosexual affair (it may have been a brief fling with the ballerina Muriel Bentley, or so she claimed), but certainly he was intimately involved with a dancer named Albia Kavan, whom he knew from both *The Great Lady* and Tamiment, from about 1939 to about 1941 or 1942, overlapping in time with several briefer but no less intense homosexual affairs. This pattern, of an announced relationship with a woman and another, generally more private one with a man—both sexual, both intensely romantic, and both involving possessiveness, jealousy, betrayal, and self-recrimination—was to persist for decades, until he finally got over the idea that he was going to conquer his gay side and settle down to married life. In the process, he left behind a string of broken engagements (with women) and broken hearts (his own and those of his romantic partners, male and female).

The 4F deferment freed Jerry to remain with Ballet Theatre throughout the war, and thus he was able to take off with the company on one of its most exciting ventures to date: a four-month stay in Mexico that began in the summer of 1942 and ended with a month of performances at the Palacio de Bellas Artes in Mexico City. The whole company delighted in the chance to get out of wartime America for a while and get away from that endless Russian dancing, and Robbins, in particular, breathed in Mexico in all its aspects. This was his second visit to the country—in the summer of 1941, Ballet Theatre had spent two months there—and each time he reveled in the culture. During his hours off from rehearsal and performance, he was painting pictures, writing stories, learning Spanish, climbing the pyramids, enjoying the local nightlife, and making notes for a play; he even directed some dance sequences for a Mexican film that Ballet Theatre participated in. Above all, he was soaking up the sounds and rhythms of Mexican dance and music, absorbing a kind of Spanish-influenced style that would repeatedly surface in the work he was later to do. And in Mexico he was also learning a new dance role, the most significant of his career to date.

Jerry was repeatedly singled out by the company's resident choreographers, who valued his verve, his intensity, his physical wit, and his quick brain even if they couldn't use him in *danseur noble* roles. Agnes de Mille cast him as a piquant figure in her *Three Virgins and a Devil* and eventually assigned him the central part of the Devil. Antony Tudor selected him for the crucial role of Benvolio in his one-act *Romeo and Juliet*, as well as parts in *Pillar of Fire*, *Goyescas*, and *Dark Elegies*. More importantly, perhaps, Tudor inspired and encouraged Robbins's own choreographic ambitions. "He would watch me in the back because I was always inventing steps and trying out lifts with the girls," Robbins later recalled. "Once at rehearsal he said, 'I'm stuck here, I need a lift. Jerry, do you have a lift for me?' I said yes. And he said, 'Oh, that's perfect. Can I have it?' And I said, 'Of course!' And I felt him giving me a pat on the back, saying, 'I believe in you.'"

Jerry's most pointed promotion as a dancer came from the Russian choreographer Michel Fokine, who had emerged from retirement to work with Ballet Theatre. Robbins performed in several of Fokine's new dances during the Mexico City season, but it was a revival of *Petrouchka*, in the title role originally made for Nijinsky, that showed what Jerry could really do. Though he had not even been cast as an understudy originally, he asked if he could learn the part on his own and was eventually rewarded with the starring role. The Russian choreographer must have recognized something in Jerry's dancing that linked him, physically and emotionally, to the lovelorn, doomed puppet who pines hopelessly for a ballerina and then is killed by his rival. Robbins himself identified with the role so closely that he connected it with a recurring dream from his adolescence. He worked and worked at the part, in Mexico and then upon his return to New York, noting in his diary that "I am and want to be humble & workmanlike before the part. It has to be good—it is me in so many ways." He even helped design the makeup for Petrouchka's face, giving himself mismatched eyebrows and a crooked mouth to show that the puppet was "badly painted" and therefore "different and 'strange.'"

To everyone's shocked dismay, Fokine died suddenly of pneumonia before ever getting to see Robbins in the role. But the ecstatic reviews that followed the September 9 Mexico premiere and the October New York performances confirmed that the aging choreographer had judged well in selecting the twenty-three-year-old Jerome Robbins for the part. "His approach was that supreme combination of mechanical and tragic that embody the argument of *Petrushka*," wrote Robert Lawrence of the *Herald Tribune*. "The drooping limbs, frustrated mask, the lightning motility that alternated with his shambling gait made this an overwhelming portrayal."

However successful he was becoming as a dancer, Robbins still longed to choreograph. From 1941 onward, he bombarded Lucia Chase with a series of complicated ideas for new dances, ranging from a full-length ballet about a legendary Southern rascal named Stack O'Lee to a multi-part family drama, *Clan Ritual*, based on his mother and her sisters. None of these got past the drawing-board stage. Then someone suggested that he focus on a shorter piece involving fewer dancers and a single set; someone else suggested he turn for inspiration to the Paul Cadmus picture *The Fleet's In*. A crowded horizontal canvas, this painting showed a collection of sailors, civilians in suits, and big-bottomed, tight-skirted women drunkenly pawing each other in a city park. "I thought, no, this is too raunchy for me,"

Robbins later recalled. "But it gave me the idea of working with sailors, which at that time were rife in New York." So as he wandered around New York, "I just kept my eyes open about what they were doing," and that enabled him to come up with both a plot and a series of gestures.

The scenario for *Fancy Free* that he handed over to Ballet Theatre in the late spring of 1943 had almost all the elements that appeared in the finished ballet when it premiered nearly a year later. The premise was that three sailors on shore leave meet up with a series of girls—first one, then another, then both together, then a different one alone, always in quantities that leave at least one sailor without a partner. The initial camaraderie among the men gives way to rivalry and eventually fisticuffs, but even the fighting is ultimately good-natured, and nothing, in the end, serves to divide the sailors up: they begin as a threesome and that's how they end. The whole thing takes place on a side-street somewhere in New York City on a hot summer night, but the street somehow becomes a bar as well, complete with a non-dancing bartender and a table for four.

The story was obviously a timely one, with the war still on and sailors still flooding the streets of New York. But that was the least of its appeal for Robbins. It was a chance for him to celebrate the city he had always loved, from the time he had been brought there as a small child for lessons—to mimic the way people walked on its streets, and met on its corners, and drank in its bars, and celebrated their poignantly quotidian lives. And it was also a way for him to commemorate and employ the warm friendships he had made among the dancers in Ballet Theatre. In the three solos he made for his two best friends in the company and himself, he celebrated the individuality of the male dancers; in their trio performances, he stressed their strong sense of unity and cohesiveness.

What is perhaps most surprising about the dance is that many of its ideas were worked out before Robbins had any

music to set it to. Yet much of the ballet's power can be attributed to a feeling that the movement springs from and is
guided by the music. The dance and its score seem completely
of a piece, with one unimaginable without the other. So it's remarkable that it wasn't until September of 1943, many months
after he had begun sketching out the piece, that Robbins first
met Leonard Bernstein. He had originally thought of asking
other composers to write a score—Marc Blitzstein was among
them, and so were Morton Gould, Lukas Foss, and Vincent
Persichetti—but none of them came through, and in the end
he was referred to a relatively obscure young man, a conductor
as well as a composer, who was living in the Carnegie Hall stu-
dios and preparing to take up a position as assistant conductor
at the Philharmonic Society of New York.

Leonard Bernstein turned out to be Robbins's musical opposite number. They were both first-generation American-born
Jews who had resisted their immigrant parents' career ambitions for them and had instead come to New York to make a
name for themselves in the arts. They were equally ambivalent
about their own homosexuality (though Bernstein, unlike Robbins, was ultimately to convert this ambivalence into a complicated marriage with children). They were almost exactly the
same age: Bernstein, born less than two months earlier, was
twenty-five on the day they met, Robbins twenty-four. They
were both slight in stature, both handsome in a clearly ethnic
way, and both convinced that they were ultimately going to
make a big difference to American culture. They were right.

As the story goes (and there is no reason to doubt it), the
aspiring choreographer simply knocked on the door of the
young composer's studio, introduced himself, and announced
that he wanted him to write the music for his first major ballet. Robbins briefly described the scenario to Bernstein, who
responded by playing a tune he had just jotted down on a paper
napkin at the Russian Tea Room that afternoon. "That's it!"

said Robbins. "That's what I had in mind!" Their collaboration began on the spot and continued over the long months when Jerry was touring the country with Ballet Theatre and meanwhile attempting to put together his own ballet. During this time the previously unknown composer became world-famous as a conductor, after he stepped in for an ailing Bruno Walter on November 14, 1943, in what became one of the most auspicious debuts ever to grace the New York musical scene. But though Bernstein's conducting responsibilities suddenly multiplied astronomically, he still continued to work on the score for Robbins's ballet.

When Robbins was dancing out of town, Bernstein would record what he had written as piano music for four hands (with his close friend Aaron Copland taking the other piano part) and send it to Jerry with warm and occasionally apologetic notes. When they were together, Jerry would stand behind Lenny at the piano, his hands on his shoulders, and viscerally let him know what kind of rhythms and melodies he wanted. Each commented on the extent to which they spoke the same language and saw things in much the same way—in part because of Jerry's own musicality and musical training, but also because Lenny had a similar sense of how the classical and the jazzy, the elegant and the popular, could intersect in American art.

After three-quarters of a century, *Fancy Free* is still a staple of the Robbins repertoire, and its many worldwide incarnations have mostly resembled the original quite closely, sometimes even exceeding it in terms of technique. But to judge by the accounts of contemporaries and the snippets of video that remain, nothing can beat the vitality and expressiveness of that first cast. At the premiere performance on April 18, 1944, the three sailors were danced by Harold Lang, John Kriza, and Jerome Robbins; the three women who sequentially encountered them were Muriel Bentley, Janet Reed, and Shirley Eckl;

and the bartender was played by the non-dancing dancer Rex Cooper.

Are there six dancers in the cast, or seven? Since there are three sailors and three women, why are there never enough women onstage to make three couples? This sense of a constant shift between odd and even, of match and mismatch, prevails throughout the dance. Nothing ever quite adds up, and something—or someone—is always left over. And this habit of keeping us off-balance, of never quite giving us what we expect, also applies to the relation between the ballet and its score. Sometimes they are exactly in sync with each other, but at other times the music goes wild while the dancers lounge about, or the dancers move across the stage while the orchestra falls silent. It is, in part, this refusal to fall into neatly aligned symmetries and predictable match-ups that makes the dance everlastingly interesting.

At the very beginning, while the curtain is still down, we hear a woman's voice singing the blues, as if on a radio or a jukebox. (Leonard Bernstein wrote this song, "Big Stuff," with Billie Holiday in mind, and in fact she was later to record it, but at the 1944 premiere the voice on the tape was that of his sister, Shirley Bernstein.) This recording, which continues briefly after the curtain rises, is suddenly interrupted by a blast of live Bernstein music, and with it three sailors in dress-white uniforms leap onto the stage, one after the other. The mood is comic and filled with joy: these guys are happy to be off the ship and out on the town, thrilled to be in a big city, and very much hoping to get laid (as they make clear in their pantomimes of a woman's hourglass figure and a sexy female walk). They are also fond of one another, taking enormous pleasure in each other's company. The sense of camaraderie is palpable, and when one leaps goofily into another's arms, or two lift the third between them, we have a sense of their profound interdependence. They are similar enough to perform steps in unison—or in canon, their other favorite mode, where each in turn repeats the previous one's gesture—but they are also distinct individuals, as their solos will eventually show.

When their first trio dance ends, they move to the bar for a drink and then stand around impatiently, waiting for some action. Eventually a woman, wearing a yellow skirt, a black jacket, and heels, slinks onto the stage behind them, her entrance introduced by a snare drum. We see her before they do (these guys are a bit oblivious, a bit too dopey to survive comfortably in the hard city, but that, of course, is part of their charm), and when they do notice her, they react like teenagers. The three sailors play keep-away with the woman's red purse, and when she tries to grab it back, they grab her in turn. This dance pitting three men against one woman is part aggression, part gentle teasing, part sexual invitation melding into sexual menace, and the score is duly complicated, mingling threatening bass notes on the piano with chirpier high notes that signal it's all in fun. Everything here depends on the power of the ballerina dancing the role: if she is strong enough (as Muriel Bentley was), she manages to retain control of the game; but if she plays it like a delicate flower, as some later ballerinas have done, the male aggressiveness can seem frightening. At the end of the sequence, when the music falls silent, she slowly and deliberately releases her arm from the nearest sailor's grasp and struts offstage on her own.

Two of the sailors follow her off, leaving the third alone to meet a new, purple-clad woman who now enters the scene. The two of them sit briefly at the bar, getting to know one another, and then they start dancing together in the ballet's sole romantic duet. The music, too, that heralds and accompanies their pairing is especially lyrical and evocative. (Sometimes what it evokes is Aaron Copland's loveliest orchestral moments, and Bernstein knew it. "There's a phrase most Aaron-like in II —I hope you don't mind. It's so pretty I can't remove it," he confessed in one of his notes to Robbins.) But this is not a normal ballet duet, with the pristine and unreachable female sought after and supported by the gallant male. Here the woman's moves are nearly as athletic as the man's. At one point, for instance, she rolls over him, her back against his bent back, and then skillfully hooks her ankle into his knee to guide herself down. Even the final lift—that gesture at which Tudor felt Robbins excelled—is hardly standard, for as he lowers her to the ground from fully extended arms, the sailor and his newfound girl gently kiss each other on the lips. This male role requires unusually good partnering skills, and it was not immodest of Jerome Robbins to assign it to himself. He was widely known as the kind of partner that gave you a sense of "real contact," noted the ballerina Sono Osato, who had been dancing with Robbins since 1941. "It wasn't the body who was just lifting you. You felt he was *there*, that he was interested."

But then, each of the three sailor roles was tailor-made for the man who danced it, as the three solos suggest. The male solos are the heart and soul of the ballet. They take place after the other two sailors have come back onstage with the original woman, and after the two women and three men have enacted various mismatches, including couple dances that repeatedly get cut into and a kind of musical chairs at the bar table. When four of the five are finally seated in the available chairs, the show-offy solos start with a bang. First up is the Harold Lang performance, which features the kind of acrobatic splits, turns, and other awe-inspiring gestures at which this dancer excelled. The second solo is much more legato, much sweeter and softer, which apparently suited the personality of John Kriza (who frequently formed an offstage trio with Muriel Bentley and Jerome Robbins, joining them at late-night bars in New Orleans or cuddling sleepily against them on the overnight train rides from one out-of-town gig to another). And finally there is the Spanish-influenced number that Robbins thought of as his

"Mexican" solo—sharp, jazzy, and sexy, with poses dramatically held and hips rhythmically swayed and bongo drums improvised on the barstool. The music for this part, a *danzón* Bernstein had borrowed from an unfinished Cuban ballet, perfectly captures Jerry's and Lenny's separate but equal love of Latin culture. (It also foreshadows, more than anything else in the entire score, the work they were later to do together on *West Side Story*.)

Soon after the end of these three terrific dances—which never fail to earn increasingly wild applause from the audience —the sailors are once again abandoned to their own devices. They moon about the stage and resume their old habits: a game of rock-scissors-paper that determines who should buy the next round of drinks (the loser is always Kriza); a chewing-gum sequence with imaginary gum but real gum-wrappers, which they throw in a distance-comparing contest; and other gestures that seem to belong more to regular life, as observed on the streets, than to ballet presented on a stage. Finally a third woman, this one dressed all in blue, emerges briefly and causes the three men to tilt sideways with desire. Then she too disappears, almost like a dream, and in the ten or fifteen remaining seconds of the dance, the music picks up and the sailors depart in the order they came in—the last one hopping as he makes the turn, like a clown doing a comic exit. And thus the circuslike mood with which the piece began is also the one that finally closes it, though a host of other complicated emotions, from staunch companionship to fresh-faced lust, from rivalry to resignation, have been raised in the intervening half-hour.

When the lights came down on that first performance in April of 1944, Robbins and his fellow dancers received an astounding twenty-two curtain calls. "It was a surprise—to all of us," Robbins recalled in an interview he gave more than forty years later. "No one had paid much attention to this ballet, so no one knew what we were doing. We were rather left alone. I think a Hurok agent came and watched it, and then went back to Hurok and said, 'I think you're in for something here.' But we didn't know that. And then the ballet opened, and we did our best, and then came that reaction, which I think was about the wildest reaction I've ever had for any ballet I've ever done."

Fancy Free was a smash hit, of the sort that ballet companies are unused to having. They hadn't expected much, so they hadn't scheduled it to be danced again for ten days—and by the time it appeared a second time, all the rave reviews had come out and the crowds were anxious to buy tickets. But only a limited amount of profit can be made, after all, from a single dance on a ballet program. And so the next thought, on the part of cannier folk in the entertainment world, was that this ballet should be converted to a Broadway show, where the aesthetic victory could be turned into a financial one.

Oliver Smith, the set designer for *Fancy Free*, was the one who came up with the idea of turning the three-sailors scenario into a Broadway musical that would come to be called *On the Town*. He enlisted a co-producer, Paul Feigay, and then persuaded Robbins and Bernstein to adapt their choreography and music to the new production, which essentially meant creating it anew. For the book and lyrics, Bernstein called on his friends Betty Comden and Adolph Green, who had never done a full musical before. Eventually they acquired a seasoned director in the form of George Abbott, who had staged *On Your Toes*, *Pal Joey*, and other Broadway successes, and under his expert guidance the show opened in New York to rave reviews on December 28, 1944.

But there were costs, and not just financial ones. In transforming itself from a ballet to a musical, the piece lost some of its free-floating, timeless charm and acquired a certain coarseness. *On the Town* is a period piece—a pleasurable period piece, with lots of great and recognizable songs, but a wartime period piece nonetheless. Gone are the shiftingly uneven numbers and fetchingly unresolvable rivalries among the principals, which made *Fancy Free* both so modern and so alluring. Instead, as Broadway tradition demanded, the three sailors got matched up neatly with three girlfriends. Nor could the musical tolerate any level of confusion or ambiguity. To distinguish among the three unnamed women who had drifted in and out of the *Fancy Free* scenario, the librettists created three "strong" characters: a tough-talking, highly sexed female taxi driver; a blue-stocking intellectual stuck with a dried-up old professor; and an ambitious, star-struck performer who gets her first break as the subway system's emblematic Miss Turnstiles. This probably seemed cute as hell and even slightly adventurous at the time, but from this distance the female roles reek of caricature and condescension. The men too suffer a loss, for the musical cannot rely on the ballet's subtle gestural language to convey both their solidarity and their independent personalities. It must instead resort to cloying songs like "Ya Got Me, Gaby," where verbal obviousness crushes what was delicate and unspoken in the dance. The biggest problem, though, is that *On the Town*, unlike *Fancy Free*, has a plot that needs to be tediously worked through. Plot is always the bane of a musical, and it is particularly tiresome in this case, when the dancing and the music are so far superior to the words.

Part of the problem, of course, comes of stretching something intended to last half an hour into the two-hour musical format. But proliferation was endemic in this production, and a big part of Abbott's job was to cut things out and rein things in. That could not have sat well with a man of Robbins's temperament—having someone else in a position of authority tell him what worked aesthetically and what didn't—and he responded by getting more and more neurotic as the rehearsals and out-of-town tryouts progressed. Of course, there was also the burden of all the investors' money that hung in the balance. Sono

Osato, the ballerina who took the lead role of Miss Turnstiles in the first incarnation of *On the Town*, later explained Jerry's anxiety by saying, "Now the money is in. It's no longer a ballet, it's money." But other aspects of the production and his role in it may have been troubling him as well.

Whatever the reason, he disappeared from the Boston tryouts for two crucial days in mid-December. After the December 13 performance—in which Osato's first-act solo "laid a big egg," according to her—no one could find Robbins anywhere. Without telling anybody, he had taken the train back to New York to consult his analyst, Dr. Frances Arkin, whom he had been seeing regularly since the success of *Fancy Free* gave him the wherewithal to begin psychoanalysis. He reappeared in Boston two days later, in time to prevent Abbott from hiring a new choreographer, and the show went on to have its great late-December triumph, giving the novice dance-maker *two* hits in a single year, one in ballet and one on Broadway. But what seemed like a satisfying resolution, almost a musical-comedy happy ending, may not have been exactly that. Success, for Robbins, carried its own toxic element, and something inside him was always impelled to resist it. "I make a disaster in order to perpetuate the feelings of inadequacy & failure projected & cursed upon me by mother and family, in order to relive time of being ousted by family," he noted after one therapy session. "I feel the veneer will come off & all will know I'm a fake & a fraud—untalented, unliked, & that the time of 'success' will be over."

Age of Anxiety

EXTERNALLY, AT ANY rate, the string of successes continued. By 1948, the year he turned thirty, Robbins had choreographed five more ballets (*Interplay, Facsimile, Pas de Trois, Summer Day,* and *Afterthought*) and four more musicals (*Billion Dollar Baby, High Button Shoes, Miss Liberty,* and *Look, Ma, I'm Dancin'!*). The winner of an entertainment-world plaque for being "Tops in Terpsichore," he was singled out by *Esquire* magazine as one of the young dance-makers to watch. And late that year, he was invited by George Balanchine and Lincoln Kirstein to join their New York City Ballet, which they had founded in 1946 under the name Ballet Society. According to Robbins, it was he who initiated the connection, after being smitten by a performance in which the nineteen-year-old Tanaquil Le Clercq danced in Balanchine's new *Symphony in C.* "I wrote to George or Lincoln or someone there, and said 'Do you need someone?'" Jerry remembered. "And they called and asked if I wanted to do a ballet, and also if I wanted to dance." Less than a year later, he himself was dancing opposite Le Clercq in the 1949 premiere of Balanchine's *Bourrée Fantasque* and also preparing to take on the main role in the revival of *Prodigal Son*. And by the fall of 1949 he had also begun work on his own first major ballet for the company: *Age of Anxiety*, a dance for four characters and background chorus, which he built in part around Tanny Le Clercq—his new best friend, his favorite muse—and himself.

The *Age of Anxiety* started life as a book-length poem by W. H. Auden, perhaps begun in response to the pacifist poet's visits to a devastated postwar Germany. Subtitled "A Baroque Eclogue," the semi-dramatic poem features four characters—three men and a woman—who speak in unrhymed lines that imitate ancient Anglo-Saxon meters, though with a freedom and a diction that is entirely modern. The four of them are strangers who meet in a Manhattan bar, where their conversation is punctuated not only by bursts of news from a nearby radio, but also by the omniscient narrator's passages in prose. The four characters go on to have various adventures in the course of a single night, including a seven-stage dream journey to an imaginary landscape and encounters with various forms of spiritual terror. They end up at the woman's flat, where she and one of the men dance together and almost go to bed together. Before this can happen, though, he falls into a drunken sleep, and the other two men disperse into the night as the woman (an English-born Jew who is a buyer at a New York department store in her daytime life) recites the *Shema Yisrael* in valediction.

As a narrative Auden's poem is almost incomprehensible, and though some of the prose passages, in particular, are remarkably insightful and moving, the poetry occasionally veers toward the ludicrous. ("My excuses throb / Louder and lamer"; "The long shadows / Disapprove of my person"; and "Reproached by the doves, / My groin groans" are the speeches spoken sequentially by three different characters in the "Seven Stages" section.) Yet the poem, published in book form in 1947, won the 1948 Pulitzer Prize, garnered its author a profile in *Time*, and was reprinted four times within its first two years.

Meanwhile, Leonard Bernstein had picked up on it almost immediately, and in April of 1949 his second symphony, *The Age of Anxiety*—a forty-minute piece which closely followed the structure of the poem—had its premiere at the Boston Symphony, with Bernstein himself performing the central piano part. It was clear that many aspects of the poem, including its overall sense of cultural anxiety, its specifically Jewish themes, and its wartime setting in New York, reverberated with the composer. And through him they just as clearly captured the imagination of his friend and collaborator Jerome Robbins.

Of the anxieties that Bernstein and Robbins shared with Auden, one was certainly over the question of sexuality. In 1946, the year he was working most intensively on the poem, W. H. Auden had the first and last sexual affair he would ever have with a woman, a Jewish American named Rhoda Jaffe whose friendship had (among other things) led him into a study of Jewish mysticism. In 1947, the year the poem came out, Leonard Bernstein, in turmoil over his own homosexuality, terminated his engagement to the actress Felicia Montealegre Cohn, the woman he would later end up marrying. And in 1948, the year *The Age of Anxiety* won the Pulitzer, the actor Montgomery Clift, concerned about his reputation and his growing career, devastated Jerome Robbins by ending their three-year relationship and moving to California. For Auden, the intertwining of questions about Jewishness with questions about his own homosexuality was simply a coincidence, but for both Bernstein and Robbins it lay at the heart of the matter. To be an acknowledged homosexual was, for each of them, to have renounced the wishes and traditions of their Jewish families— to have "betrayed the Poppa, the Jewish Poppas" in order to live as an artist and hold onto "all that I had gained, gotten, achieved, changed," as Robbins put it toward the end of his life.

For Robbins, the Auden poem must have set off other emotional echoes as well. Though the music may have been what drew him to the project, he resorted to the actual text in creating and rehearsing his new ballet, requiring all the main dancers (Todd Bolender, Francisco Moncion, and Tanaquil Le Clercq, in addition to himself) to read the whole book. He had gone through his own copy in detail, underlining certain passages and making marginal notes next to others. Robbins would have been especially intrigued by the initial lines of the first speaking character, who looks into the mirror that faces his barstool and says:

> My deuce, my double, my dear image,
> Is it lively there, that land of glass
> Where song is a grimace, sound logic
> A suite of gestures?

As the prose narrator explains to us, this character "caught the familiar eye of his reflection in the mirror behind the bar and wondered why he was still so interested in that tired old widower who would never be more now than a clerk in a shipping office. . . . More, that is, as a public figure: for as so often happens in the modern world—and how much restlessness, envy and self-contempt it causes—there was no one-to-one correspondence between his social or economic position and his private mental life."

That, in a nutshell, summarized Jerry Robbins's repeated problem: the struggle he was constantly engaged in between the "veneer" of accumulated success and the true self that lay underneath it, "untalented, unliked." And to have Auden couch the problem in terms of a glance in the mirror would have struck him as nearly uncanny, given his own lifelong obsessions with mirrors and masks, going all the way back to his adolescent multiple "selves" with their "blank vacant eyes." So it almost seems over-determined that those same masks, though eyeless this time, would make an appearance in Robbins's *Age of Anxiety* (from whose title, characteristically, he had dropped both Auden's and Bernstein's definite article).

It's not possible, from this distance in time, to get a real sense of what the ballet was like. Very little evidence of it remains, other than anecdotes by cast members and a few minutes of silent film footage. Unlike *Fancy Free*, it was not a ballet that stayed in the repertoire, and its existence is so generally forgotten that when the Royal Ballet choreographer Liam Scarlett recently choreographed his own *Age of Anxiety* ballet to the Bernstein score, no mention was made of the Robbins predecessor. But in one of the very few snippets of Robbins's dance that has been preserved on film, one can see those eyeless white masks. They are fencing masks, apparently, and they completely cover the faces of the dancers who surround the central four, creating an aura of inhuman threat and emotional emptiness. It is a fearsome image, a concrete evocation of all the inchoate terrors alluded to in Auden's poem and magnified by the power of Bernstein's music—and it is also a very Jerome Robbins image, suggesting as it does a deep suspicion about the very idea of a self.

At the time of its premiere, *Age of Anxiety* met with a strong response. The audiences who saw it during its initial performances in February and March of 1950 were enthusiastic; George Balanchine apparently considered it a fitting follow-up to his own *Prodigal Son* revival that season; and *Dance Magazine* even gave it a choreography award. The critical response was cautious but mainly positive, with critic John Martin exemplifying the general trend when he said that though the ballet was "quite as obscure as Auden's poem and just as unavoidably unresolved," it was also Robbins's "most profound and provocative assignment" to date, a "fascinating" dance from a choreographer whose "intuition is uncannily penetrating" and whose "emotional integrity is unassailable."

But Robbins's integrity—emotional or otherwise—was precisely the quality that at that very moment was in the process of being assailed. For even as he was putting the finishing touches on his new ballet, he learned from his agent that his scheduled Easter appearance on Ed Sullivan's *Toast of the Town* television show had been abruptly canceled. The reason? It was his old membership in the Communist Party, which he had joined in the early 1940s, along with his sister, Sonia, and many of their friends. Now the notoriously Red-baiting Ed Sullivan was threatening to expose him, not only as a Communist but also as a homosexual, if he didn't name names and cooperate with Joseph McCarthy's ever-growing investigation. Robbins finessed the issue this time by meeting briefly and privately with Sullivan; then, when the FBI got involved, he called in his lawyers before disappearing on a long European tour. But the game of evasion that began for him in early 1950 was to end three years later with his testimony before the House Un-American Activities Committee—a capitulation that, in his own mind as well as others', he never managed to live down.

It's not as if Jerry was the only figure in the arts world under political fire. Leonard Bernstein had been splashed across the pages of *Life* magazine only a few days after his own *Age of Anxiety* premiere, his photo displayed among those of fifty or so prominent Americans who had recently attended the Cultural Conference for World Peace held at New York's Waldorf-Astoria. "Dupes and Fellow Travellers Dress Up Communist Fronts" read the headline over the assembled portraits of Arthur Miller, Lillian Hellman, Charlie Chaplin, Albert Einstein, Norman Mailer, Clifford Odets, Aaron Copland, and other cultural eminences at whom *Life* was pointing an accusing finger. Most people in the entertainment world resisted the pressure to testify against their fellow left-wingers, even when it meant losing out on opportunities that mattered to them. In Bernstein's case, for instance, his political affiliation may have been what cost him the conductorship of the Boston Symphony Orchestra. It's certainly what prevented him from appearing onstage next to President Truman at a 1949 event honoring Chaim Weizmann, Israel's first president.

Robbins, though, took the threats of exposure more seriously than most. Perhaps because his choreographic career was on such a steep rise—or perhaps, conversely, because he felt he had such a tenuous grasp on the success he was manifestly having—he was terrified of what he would be left with if it were all taken away. The generalized Age of Anxiety that afflicted America in this period was for him a very specific anxiety about the evanescence of external achievements. To have his career ruined would be, for Jerry, to lose his entire sense of himself: if he was not his achievements, he was nothing. He felt this intensely in 1950, and he was still feeling it over forty years later when he attempted to finish his guilt-ridden autobiographical play, *The Poppa Piece*. It was fear of being turned back into his father, of becoming "no one, like *him*," that motivated him "to betray the Poppas," he said in a notebook entry; and what had set this fear off was his sense that the work "which gave me my public identity was at stake."

Throughout 1951 and 1952, while others in the entertainment world lost their jobs and in some cases went to jail, Robbins continued to play footsie with McCarthy's minions. In March of 1951, when his tremendously successful choreography for *The King and I* was about to open on Broadway and Hollywood was beckoning with possible scripts for him to direct, Ed Sullivan—this time in his capacity as a newspaper columnist—fired another blast. "Tip to Red Probers: Subpena Jerome Robbins" was the headline of Sullivan's March 24 front-page column in the *Philadelphia Inquirer* (spelling apparently not being among his, or the newspaper's, strong points). He went on to repeat the solecism in his sentence urging "that the House Un-American Activities Committee subpena ballet star and choreographer Jerome Robbins. . . . In my office not long ago, Robbins revealed that he had been a card-member of the Communist Party. . . . He has a wide familiarity with Commies of all hues."

Robbins, terrified, immediately sublet his apartment and again fled New York for a long stay in Europe. His political fate, meanwhile, rested in the hands of a lawyer, Robert Lawrence Siegel, who apparently spoke to the FBI on Jerry's behalf in April. Siegel, the FBI report said, "stated that the subject had told him things and wanted to be reinterviewed by the FBI to furnish information about his Communist Party activities that he had not mentioned on 4/25/50." But Robbins, safely tucked away in Europe and then Israel, was out of reach of the Committee for the whole summer. Via his lawyers, he learned that HUAC had announced that its session starting on September 17th would be its last. He began to make plans for his return, and by the end of October he was back in New York, working for minimum dancer's wage at New York City Ballet while receiving hundreds of dollars in royalties every week from *The King and I.*

The relatively low profile may have protected him at first. Throughout 1952 he produced a series of works for the New York City Ballet while also being tapped occasionally to repair the dancing in Broadway shows. (He himself had stopped performing in mid-1952, deciding henceforth to pour all of his talents into choreography and, he hoped, directing.) But that surreptitious strategy only worked for a while. Just as he was putting his uncredited finishing touches on the Boston tryouts of *Wonderful Town,* the boom he had been waiting for was finally lowered. Early in 1953, he was summoned to a closed-door session of HUAC, which had not, as forecast, stopped its hearings, but had actually increased their number and reach since late 1951. This was duly followed, on May 5, 1953, with his testimony as a "friendly witness" at a special New York session of HUAC, held at the U.S. Courthouse in Foley Square.

Robbins's lawyer, Lawrence Siegel, sat beside him during his hour of testimony, but it was Jerry who had to answer the questions raised by the committee members. After a polite exchange about his own artistic work as a choreographer, they asked when he had first joined the Communist Party, and why. What had been its effect on him? Had the Communists forced him to shape his art in certain ways? What caused him to leave the Party in 1947? But they were not just interested in him. After all, his "card-member" status had already been confirmed in earlier testimony. What they wanted was for him to name names, and Robbins seemed almost too eager to do it. The list came pouring out: Lettie Stever, Lloyd Gough, Madeleine Lee, Elliot Sullivan, Jerome Chodorov, Edward Chodorov, Edna Ocko, Lionel Berman . . . Many of these were his colleagues in the theater world; some were longtime friends. When he was finished, the congressmen on the committee congratulated him on his openness and helpfulness: "I am going to see *The King and I* tonight, and I will appreciate it much more," one of them fawningly remarked. They urged him to make a final statement about why he had bravely testified before HUAC, despite the obvious risk of being called a stool pigeon, and Robbins obediently answered, "I think I made a great mistake in entering the Communist Party, and I feel that I am doing the right thing as an American."

Later that day, according to an account by the scriptwriter Arthur Laurents, Jerry said, "I'll never know for years whether I did the right thing." By the time he reported this, Laurents had become one of Robbins's most outspoken antagonists, so the whole story needs to be taken with a grain of salt. But in any case, what he most clearly remembered was his own response.

"No, I can tell you right now," Laurents answered him. "You were a shit."

Many agreed with that assessment, including some who were very close to Robbins. Sonia and her husband, George Cullinen, wouldn't speak to him for years, and a cousin, Bob Silverman, cut him off forever. The friends he had named, and even the more distant acquaintances, never forgave him. "Stabbed by the wicked fairy" was Edward Chodorov's acerbic if somewhat homophobic assessment. And even those he had not personally injured viewed him from then on as a traitor, an informer. When, years later, he ran into Zero Mostel on the rehearsal set of the 1962 musical *A Funny Thing Happened on the Way to the Forum* (Robbins had been called in as script-doctor to save the show), the blacklisted comic greeted him in front of the rest of the cast by saying, "Hiya, loose lips!" Jerry's laughter in response, though it was taken as a purposeful ice-breaker, could have been the result of shock, or even guilt. Probably it was a combination of all three.

Certainly guilt was an ever-present feature of his own memories of the event. From 1975, when he first began working on what was eventually *The Poppa Piece* (which in Robbins's earliest notes was called "The Jew Piece"), to 1991, when he attempted a partial staging of this permanently uncompleted and probably uncompletable work, Jerry struggled to integrate his feelings about his HUAC behavior with all the other kinds of betrayal he felt guilty about. He wrote and rewrote his version of the testimony scene, never to his own satisfaction. He was trying to show that his fears of being exposed—of being dragged back to the nothing that he inherently felt himself to be—motivated and explained his HUAC betrayal. But he couldn't do this without seeming to justify himself, to blame the Poppa that stood behind and to the side of his actions. In one draft, he has the Poppa of the piece, a character named Herschel Vitkowitz, present in the courtroom scene as a representative of both Jewish tradition and ethical responsibility, while his son, Jake, answers the committee's questions. As the father urges the son not to name names, Jake responds, "You want to drag me back to where you are. They're gonna take it all away." And then he points to Herschel and says to the committee members, "Take him!"

A year after essentially giving up on *The Poppa Piece*, Robbins returned to it in one final notebook entry. "One of the keenest feelings," he said about his HUAC testimony, "is that I betrayed the Poppa—the Jewish Poppas." His career, his achievements, what he called his "public identity," was everything to him, and "To sacrifice for it I had to betray the Poppas." But it was a temporary solution only, raising further and more complicated problems over the course of a lifetime. "This rupture of all respect for myself & my denial of my father stuck with me—haunted me," Robbins wrote in 1992, when he was seventy-four years old. Even if others could have forgiven him for his HUAC testimony, he would never be able to forgive himself.

And this bundle of guilt became all-inclusive. For Jerome Robbins, the multitude of things he had been fleeing from for years—his own Jewishness, his father's humdrum life, his conflicted sexuality, his Communism, his anti-Communism, his lifelong sense of being an emptiness covered by a mask—all became tangled up together in one great self-condemnation. "I accuse" had been the first two words of Ed Sullivan's 1951 "Tip to Red Probers" *Inquirer* column. But no accusation leveled by anyone else in public could ever have the continuing power of the one Robbins internally brought against himself.

The King and I

By 1951 HE had been involved in a number of Broadway successes, but this was to be his biggest one to date. For one thing, he was choreographing for the first time for Richard Rodgers and Oscar Hammerstein II, the duo who had already produced *Oklahoma!* and *South Pacific.* Rodgers & Hammerstein were pushing the limits of what the musical comedy could be, allowing it to have a darker side than its label would suggest, and that appealed immensely to Jerome Robbins. He was also pleased to be working on a big-budget production, with a salary that seriously augmented his low-paying ballet work. Perhaps best of all, he would be allowed to explore and develop a new style of dance, a fusion between Eastern and Western modes.

The King and I, loosely based on the biography of the Victorian Englishwoman who served as governess to the children of the King of Siam, was not just set in Siam. It was also intended to feature Siamese-style music and Siamese-style dance (or at least a Western approximation of these things). In preparation for this work, Robbins avidly researched and examined Southeast Asian court dances as well as other kinds of dancing from Cambodia, Laos, India, Japan, and elsewhere. When it came time to train the dancers in the *King and I* company, he put them through many hours of technical rehearsals, at which they learned to mimic the unfamiliar gestures—flexed feet, extended fingers, and so on—that characterized these forms of dance. He also gave them exercises that were meant to develop their characters as well as their style. "You are born dancers in the royal palace, from generation to generation, an honored family of dancers," he told the members of the chorus. "So whatever you do has *dignity*."

The music for most of his work had been set in advance by the Rodgers score, which came to Robbins complete with songs like "Shall We Dance?" and instrumental numbers like "March of the Siamese Children." What he made of them, though, was beyond expectations. The polka of "Shall We Dance?" (performed in the original stage version by Gertrude Lawrence and Yul Brynner, and then by Brynner and Deborah Kerr for the subsequent film) is one of the most memorable dances for nondancers ever created. It cements our sense of the semi-erotic, semi-formal, collaborative yet willful connection between the governess, Anna Leonowens, and her employer, the King; in that sense, it has a character-creating and plot-furthering function in the musical. But it also, no less importantly, lends the whole production a moment of sheer joy. You cannot watch this sequence, either as a child or as an adult, without wanting to jump up and perform a polka yourself, and you cannot see the dance and hear its closely matching tune without having them stick with you forever.

"March of the Siamese Children" is only slightly less enrapturing. It introduces each of the King's many children to

Anna (and to the audience) in a parade of steps that is simultaneously very restricted and individually appealing. This was the first time Robbins had ever worked with children, and by all accounts he loved them, and they him; there were none of the angry blow-ups that marked his rehearsals with adults. He gave each child a special element of choreography to crown his or her little moment in the limelight, and whereas the near-repetition could have become boring in other hands, here it has a sense of inevitability combined with surprise: precisely what one hopes for from a combination of Eastern rigor and Western individualism. In its own way, the "March" is yet another expression of the coming-together of Anna and the King, a meeting-ground of two disparate cultures that are nonetheless able to sense each other's feelings.

Perhaps the segment for which Robbins became most famous, though, was the dance number "The Small House of Uncle Thomas." A Siamese-style exposition of the *Uncle Tom's Cabin* plot, intended by Hammerstein as a way of mirroring the King's own abuses of power, this lengthy piece at first gave Robbins a great deal of trouble, and he found himself repeatedly stymied. Then, with the help of Trude Rittman (who had been assigned as his dance arranger), he came up with a series of solos, group dances, and staging effects that evocatively conveyed the story. Some of this required new music, which Rittman composed; other parts demanded new dialogue, which Robbins supplied. "It was an enormous challenge for both of us," Rittman said later. "He kept saying, 'We are like a very, very old couple going up a steep hill. One is pushing the other.'"

To a modern eye, the originality of the choreography may be outweighed at times by its slightly embarrassing Orientalism. This is Asian-style movement as envisioned by an obviously Western mind, and at times the vaguely Chinese-y becomes positively cheesy. The clever use of masks, though, and the brilliantly designed "river" made of fabric are as powerful and striking as they ever were; and if some of the lyrics seem a little hokey ("Run, Liza, run, run, run!"), the overall tone of menace is still there. Certainly the reviewers who attended the March 29, 1951 premiere of *The King and I* noticed no such drawbacks. They pronounced the choreography a complete success, and the *Times* theater critic, Brooks Atkinson, singled out "The Small House of Uncle Thomas" in particular as "a stunning ballet that seasons the liquid formalism of Eastern dancing with some American humor."

The Siamese setting would have seemed distant and unfamiliar to Robbins, but everything else about *The King and I* drew on experiences much closer to home. A benevolent dictator —foreign-born, aristocratic—who ruled his little kingdom unopposed, took brides from among the available beauties in his court, and attempted to destroy any man who would steal one of his potential concubines: did this not ring a bell for a member of George Balanchine's ballet troupe? Some of the events that would make Balanchine resemble the King of Siam were yet to occur (it was not until 1969, for instance, that he banished his adored Suzanne Farrell and her new husband, Paul Mejia, from his New York City Ballet court), but enough parallels existed by 1951 to make the analogy credible. Like the king, Balanchine had excellent manners, honed over generations of courtly upbringing, that masked an iron will. Like the Siamese monarch, he spoke an accented English filled with charming and perhaps, at times, even purposeful errors. Like the Rodgers & Hammerstein character, he was interested in other cultures than his own, other ways of doing things, but only if they did not conflict with his inherent beliefs in his pre-eminent rightness—a rightness which was affirmed by everyone around him, since the entire dance world echoed his high opinion of his own stature. Like the king in his harem, he surrounded himself with beautiful women and viewed each one of them as a potential sexual conquest, while also admiring them as aesthetic objects that lent power and purpose to his reign. "Ballet is woman," Balanchine famously remarked, and this seeming praise of the softer sex contained its own darker side, its own clue to his pasha-like behavior.

Balanchine was certainly not the only ballet-master who behaved in this way. In fact, the history of professional dance companies is a history of favoritism, sexual intrigue, and wounded jealousy. This goes back at least to Vaslav Nijinsky and his director-manager, Sergei Diaghilev, and forward to the latest modern dance company in which the lead dancer is married to the director-choreographer. It crosses gender boundaries and preference boundaries: a heterosexual company director is neither more nor less likely than a homosexual one to exploit his dancers sexually, and female choreographers can be as predatory as their male counterparts. Nor is this something that can simply be legislated against. Controlling sexual desire is really not viable in an art form which depends so heavily on the unique capacities of human bodies, their highly attractive physical appearance, the routine intimacy of constant touching, and the whims of personal taste. In fact, some of the same whims that cause love affairs can also cause great dances—there's just no getting around that, and to prevent the choreographer from selecting his dancers on the basis of his passions is to dam up a crucial source of the art form.

Jerry Robbins, like everyone else in the world of dance, understood this, and though he was not particularly predatory himself, he did cast his friends (some of whom were also his lovers) in roles that he designed around them. He adhered to the idea that the choreographer is, to a certain extent, a king. But he also realized that in the company he had chosen to join in late 1948, there could really only be one true ruler. So Jerry, like Anna in Siam, was a governess who didn't really have the power to govern. He was invariably going to be a secondary figure in the New York City Ballet, and it was part of the complexity of his personality that he accepted this. For he, too, worshipped Balanchine. "When I watch Balanchine work, it's so extraordinary I want to give up," he wrote in his journal in 1971, nearly a quarter-century after he had begun to live and work under the other man's dominance.

"From the very beginning, Balanchine was what he wanted to be," one of his Ballet Theatre colleagues, Isabel Brown, later recalled. Robbins himself remembered an important conversation with Balanchine that took place before they ever started to work together, probably in the summer of 1945, a year after the premiere of *Fancy Free*. Jerry noted that at that time "my approach toward ballet was very dramatic, theatrical, concentrated, and I felt that anything at all could be told by dance." But Balanchine said to him, "Well, it doesn't have to be so theatrical," and then went on:

> There's a stage; it's empty. Four girls come on and dance with one boy. They go off and leave him alone. It's theatrical. . . . Then six girls come on and dance on the other side. That's theatrical. And then two people do a solo, and it's just two people who are dancing and then they go off. And that's already theatre and entertainment.

For Robbins, the moment was revelatory, and lasting. "It was just like the light had been turned on about what choreography was really *about*," Jerry commented. And this sense of enlarged perspective that he found in Balanchine's work continued to enchant him, even when he encountered it in other art forms. "He's so cool—so objective—he's like Balanchine," he was to write years later about the painter Piero della Francesca.

Still, the differences between Robbins's and Balanchine's choreography tended over the course of their careers to hinge on this opposition between dramatic character, on the one hand,

and abstract elegance, on the other. When Balanchine asked Robbins to help him with the company's new *Nutcracker* in 1954, for instance, it was the mouse battle between children and adults he gave him—as if expecting Jerry to reproduce the kind of appeal he had brought to the children's dance in *The King and I*, where individual character and gentle humor prevailed over dance skill. In that same year, when Robbins wanted the company to take on *The Dybbuk*, with choreography by him and music by Leonard Bernstein, both Balanchine and his sidekick Lincoln Kirstein flatly turned him down, on the grounds that New York City Ballet was not the right place for such a plot-driven dance. Balanchine had, in working with his dancers, "eliminated almost all personality . . . substituting instead,—elegance, clarity, balance and good manners," Kirstein wrote in his explanation of this decision. He suggested that Robbins and Bernstein instead consider taking the dance to an Israeli modern dance company—a veiled insult that Robbins was quick to perceive as such.

The presence of Kirstein complicated the relationship between Balanchine and Robbins, even as it superficially seemed to ease it. On the surface, Lincoln Kirstein was much more like Jerome Robbins: he was American, he was Jewish, he was homosexual . . . But perhaps these very similarities caused Kirstein to want to keep his distance from the relative upstart. It was Kirstein's private fortune (emanating from Filene's department store in Boston) that had enabled Balanchine to found his dance company in 1946, and though other sources of funding soon became necessary, Lincoln Kirstein retained his important role as co-founder and constant advisor. On the surface, he was in favor of having Robbins join the company as associate artistic director, and he seductively drew him back whenever Jerry seemed tempted to leave. "You are the only choreographer that the country has produced who has the equivalent authority as Balanchine," he wrote during Jerry's 1951 HUAC-induced escape to Europe, "and you will have to replace him when he is absent, incapacitated, or dead. I realize the responsibility but our talents do not entirely belong to us, nor do we choose them; they find us. In your case, Balanchine considers you are the only person whom he wants to work with."

And work together they did, occupying a shared office at New York City Ballet and even collaborating at times on specific dances. Soon after joining the company, Robbins paired with Balanchine to create a forgettable dance called *Jones Beach*—something light and frothy, set to a contemporary score, that was obviously meant to make use of Jerry's "American" qualities. Later Jerry contributed his mouse-battle section to *Nutcracker*, and still later, Balanchine attempted to make a contribution to Robbins's *Fanfare*. This was on a day when Jerry couldn't appear at rehearsal and had asked Mr. B. to take his place. Apparently Balanchine exceeded his brief, taking the dance past the point where Robbins had left it. Jerry returned to find dancing-in-unison where he had instead intended to use counterpoint, and he canceled Balanchine's instructions. "I fixed, but you changed," Mr. B. reminded him whenever *Fanfare* was performed. This little setback did not, however, stop their collaboration. Years later, for the 1972 Stravinsky Festival, they jointly choreographed *Pulcinella* as well as dancing in it together as two beggars. Violette Verdy, who was a member of the company at the time, took this as "a little wink at some of the critics" who thought the two New York City Ballet choreographers were in competition with each other. Instead, Verdy felt, they were co-conspirators: "They were plotting together."

Still, the difference in their informal titles—"Jerry" and "Mr. B."—was indicative of their stature among the company members. Balanchine was the revered choreographer; Jerry was a fellow dancer who had somehow been promoted to this higher realm. The dancers acknowledged his talents but also felt able to resent him, for he was just a human being on their level, not a god. (Jerry, by the way, not only understood but also shared this worshipful attitude. "He is my ideal too. I adore him as a person, and he is my God as an artist," Robbins once wrote about Balanchine in a letter to Tanaquil Le Clercq.)

In his characteristic way, Jerry occasionally did things to further the dancers' resentment. Whereas Balanchine was invariably polite in rehearsals, Jerry could lose his temper and make people feel terrible. In other ways, too, his rehearsals were psychologically more demanding than Balanchine's. Several dancers recalled that though Mr. B.'s sessions could be harder technically, Jerry's rehearsals put you through the emotional wringer, always demanding a certain degree of self-exposure. Others pointed out that because of his unending perfectionism, Jerome Robbins rehearsed forever, compared to Balanchine. "I have never spent so many hours rehearsing such a short little pas de deux," said Peter Martins of his role in one Robbins dance. "It drove me mad. I was used to Mr. B. I mean, Balanchine would make a ballet in two rehearsals in the practice room." But for Jerry's little duet, "I was like two months in the main hall with Violette." For the most part, the dancers sensed that both the prolonged perfectionism and the bad manners stemmed from Jerry's insecurities. But that didn't necessarily make his behavior any easier to take.

On the other hand, Robbins could be lovable and kind if he liked you, and he was obviously more accessible, more of a regular guy than Balanchine was. Still, it didn't pay to cross him in any way. "Maybe there was more fear toward Jerry," said Martins (who, as the man who ultimately took over the company after Balanchine died, may not have been the most disinterested source). "Not that there wasn't fear with Balanchine, but it was a different kind of fear. It was more of an aura."

That aura was, in part, what allowed George Balanchine to attract the remarkable ballerinas who became his wives or, in later years, his muses. When Jerry first joined the company, Balanchine was married to Maria Tallchief, his third dancer-wife, who performed in a number of leading roles at New York City Ballet, including opposite Robbins in the revival of *Prodigal Son*. But by the middle of 1951, that marriage had fallen apart, and the forty-seven-year-old Balanchine had taken up with his newest protégé, twenty-one-year-old Tanaquil Le Clercq.

That she was also Robbins's inspiration and intimate friend created some serious problems. Jerry became very upset when he learned that Tanny had chosen George over him. The letter he wrote to her from Europe has been lost, but the one in which she answered him remains. "I just love you, to talk to, to go around with, play games, laugh like hell, etc.," she explained. "However I'm in love with George—Maybe it's a case of he got here first—Maybe not—I don't know—anyway I'm staying with him. Can't we be friends? Like they say in the movies."

Robbins was already feeling persecuted that summer by the McCarthy witch-hunt, and now he had yet another reason to steer clear of New York. He threw himself into a major new love affair with a male dancer, Buzz Miller, and lingered for months in Paris. Even after Buzz left to return to America, Jerry stayed on, resisting Lincoln Kirstein's strenuous attempts to get him back. "Balanchine wants to give you more authority if you can be counted on to want to take it," Kirstein offered, and then followed this up with some excessive praise (excessive, that is, compared to the denigrating remarks he had made about Robbins in his letters to other people):

> I believe you are the only choreographer alive who can take George's place; historically speaking you are not as fortunate as he; he was a classic dancer, trained under the Empire and the early USSR, and he had Diaghilev, and you alas, have

only me; but what is more important, you are an American
with an amazing gift for gesture; no one else has it.

Even this, though, was not enough to get Jerry back to New
York. It may have been another letter from Tanny that finally
provoked his return. "I think you stink," she wrote him.

> If you are sick why don't you come back? . . . If you can't
> dance you could at least come back and help—my god,
> you have your name on the program as doing something—
> You are a wonderful dancer and you never dance—The
> best young choreographer and never choreograph—What
> the hell goes on? . . . Can't you think of anything besides
> yourself—What about Til—George wanted it for you. . . . I
> really don't understand you. I think you are an S.O.B.

And she signed off by saying, "I'm sorry if this makes you *so*
mad you won't write to me, I wish you would just explain—I'm
understanding but to a point—Love, Tan."

Whether it was out of his feelings of obligation to Tanny
or to George, or some combination of both, this note appears
to have done the trick. He returned to New York less than a
month after receiving it and began to work on the *Tyl Ulen-
spiegel* that Balanchine choreographed around him. The new
piece drew heavily on Jerry's talents as an expressive dancer,
and he was reportedly thrilled to be working with Balanchine
again. But he soon wearied of his role as a company dancer,
especially when the New York City Ballet went on tour in the
summer of 1952. Forced to leave behind Buzz Miller (with
whom he was now living in New York) and faced with the dis-
comforts of a traveling dancer, he complained about the fact
that Balanchine's name, and his alone, was "plastered all over,"
even though several Robbins dances were also on the program.
As he wrote to his friend Robert Fizdale, a musician back in
New York:

I hated being a member of a traveling company again—I resented the whole thing & felt it completely degrading to stand in line for money, pick up and return shoe bags & costumes, get assigned a dressing room that was poor, etc. etc. As a matter of fact, I've so hated dancing that I've spoken to George, & I am coming out of Bouree and Piper & will only dance Tyl as there is no replacement for me—& Anxiety.

At the age of nearly thirty-four, Robbins had not outgrown dancing in a physical sense: he was still young enough to perform all his roles well. But he had outgrown it as a man. He could no longer tolerate the loss of status it implied, compared to the attention and, yes, wealth that he could earn as a choreographer. So when he returned to New York in the fall of 1952, he gave up on dancing entirely and took on a Broadway show, *Two's Company*, which starred Bette Davis. That the show turned out to be a flop ("Bette Davis in *Two's Company* is like hearing the Fifth Symphony played on a comb," wrote Walter Kerr in the *Times*) was less important than that it had gotten Robbins back into choreographing. By the time *Two's Company* opened on Broadway in December of 1952, he was already working on two new dances for the upcoming spring season of the New York City Ballet.

For personal and professional reasons, Robbins didn't have much to do with the New York City Ballet between 1957 and 1969. He had plenty of Broadway successes during that period, including major ones with *West Side Story, Peter Pan, Fiddler on the Roof*, and *Gypsy*, and he was finally allowed to direct as well as choreograph—not only on the New York stage, but also in Hollywood. He worked on straight plays as well as musicals, and as part of his exploration of the drama, he undertook a multi-year experimental project called American Theatre Lab. For a time he even had his own touring dance company, Ballets: USA, which spent substantial periods in Europe, as did he.

And in a brief return to his old company, Lucia Chase's Ballet Theatre, he staged a version of *Les Noces*, using Stravinsky's original score but completely reinventing the choreography.

Over the years, Lincoln Kirstein had issued more than one invitation for him to do a new ballet for NYCB, and Robbins had maintained friendly ties with the company, occasionally coming back to teach new dancers the parts in his old dances. Now, in 1969, Kirstein invited him to become involved in City Center's twenty-fifth anniversary gala, and he said yes. As Robbins later recalled it, a big part of his motivation was the chance to re-enter Balanchine's realm. "The master choreographer was working there," he commented, "and what more pleasure and education could you want?"

It was a critical time for the New York City Ballet. Balanchine, now sixty-five, had fallen in love with Suzanne Farrell and had divorced Tanaquil Le Clercq so as to be free to remarry, but the twenty-something Farrell, although happy to dance the roles he made for her, did not want anything to do with him sexually. The effect was to heighten Balanchine's obsession with this unobtainable muse, and many of his old dancers were threatening to leave. ("I don't mind being listed alphabetically, but I do mind being treated alphabetically," Maria Tallchief reportedly said.) Jerry's return was thus a lifesaver for the company, and he sensed their gratitude in the collective response to the first new dance he made for them, a piece called *Dances at a Gathering* that was set to the piano music of Chopin. It premiered at a gala on May 8, 1969, the same day Balanchine informed Suzanne Farrell and the young dancer she had recently married, Paul Mejia, that they were no longer working at New York City Ballet.

Balanchine eventually recovered from this fit of pique, and Farrell even came back to the company to dance during his last few years. But what ensued in the short term was a slight shift in power, at a moment when the weakened King desperately needed his Governess to lend stability and vitality to the company. This Robbins did, producing a series of dances that combined his old love of theatricality with a new sense of musicality and dance-for-its-own-sake. He followed up *Dances at a Gathering* with another piece set to Chopin, *In the Night*, and then with the brilliant, Bach-inspired *Goldberg Variations*.

But in the time Robbins had been away from the company, the ballet world had changed. Mainly because of Balanchine and his remarkable achievements in the form, ballet had become *the* performance art for the New York intelligentsia. In-the-know audiences flocked to his premieres and avidly talked about them afterward, gossiping about his ballerinas even as they also commented on his inventive choreography. Led by the high priestess of their cult, Arlene Croce, these balleto-manes elevated the Balanchine aesthetic to the pinnacle position, with every other choreographer falling lower on the scale. So to the extent Robbins differed from Balanchine in the way he approached ballet (and he always had differed and always would, despite his worshipful admiration), he was considered an inferior artist. Precisely the things that made him unique as a choreographer—the modern, folk, and even street-style gestures that he added to his ballets; the function of plot and character in his works; the presence of humor and gentle self-mockery in his dances; even the fact that his women were not elongated, rarefied, unobtainable muses, but strong, feisty dancers equivalent to the men—defined him as a second-rater.

"A lot of people said it was like Balanchine was the Met and Jerome Robbins was City Opera," said the choreographer Mark Morris, who came to New York in the 1970s. "And a lot of people's husbands would go to City Ballet because of the Robbins; the Balanchine was too much for them, too many tights, too complicated."

Robbins, though he was happy to be popular with the

masses, was wounded at the tone of the ballet reviews. The general implication on the part of dance critics and dyed-in-the-wool ballet fans was that Jerome Robbins was excellent at Broadway work and distinctly less good at choreographing ballets. They couldn't credit that anything so unBalanchinian might be making its own kind of aesthetic demands on them, and they measured everything he did against the yardstick of the Master's work. Even a piece like *The Goldberg Variations*, which might have been expected to impress those who liked sensuous abstraction and acute musicality, was greeted by Arlene Croce as "ninety minutes at hard labor."

Shortly after the May 1971 *Goldberg* premiere, Robbins began working on a new dance called *Watermill*. It was a highly personal, self-revealing piece, one that would eventually earn him the most cutting Arlene Croce review of his career. "If it really is the personal testament that its admirers take it for—personal in the sense of autobiographical—then it is even worse than I think it is," she wrote in *Ballet Review*. "I believe he is fatally attracted to pretentious undertakings. . . . The man is like a Houdini of stagecraft, and he seems to have grown tired of his magic, tired or afraid." But even before this cruel review appeared, when he was still putting *Watermill* together, Jerry was aware of the anxiety he was experiencing over the new work. He had one of those nakedness dreams associated with self-exposure, a dream in which he experienced "much anxiety about being lost, or rather stranded, in the hands of strangers in a foreign land, with no money . . . and no clothes." The only thing he had with which to cover himself was an enormous overcoat, obviously belonging to someone much larger than himself. "Then came the revelation—I *want* to lose my clothes—I want to get rid of my OVER COAT—*take off the coating*—but I have great anxiety about it," he noted to himself.

As he analyzed it in his journal, the dream seemed to be

once again about his usual anxieties: that is, the overwhelming role that his external achievements played in his own sense of identity, and his feeling that he would be reduced to nothing if he did not have this "coating." And clearly this fear of loss, this dread of being uncovered, is indeed there in his account. But the dream itself, especially in his written rendering of it, also points to something else—his wish, his active *desire* to rid himself of the too-large overcoat and stand on his own, even if that means he must stand naked.

Anyone who knows anything about nineteenth-century Russian literature (and Robbins was a highly literate man, well versed in Russian culture) will recall that Nikolai Gogol famously wrote a short story called "The Overcoat." It is a tale about status, and yearning, and humiliation, and loss. In its own time, it was such an influential work that Dostoyevsky reportedly said about the subsequent generation of Russian writers, "We all come out from Gogol's overcoat."

Behind Jerome Robbins, too, stood a towering Russian figure, an enormous presence whom he considered in every way larger than himself. On some level, conscious or unconscious, Robbins may well have felt that at least as a choreographer, and possibly as a man, he was eternally in the process of emerging from Balanchine's overcoat. His dream told him he wanted to escape from this powerful influence, but in his waking life he apparently wanted it both ways. And Robbins continued to have it both ways, sharing choreographic responsibility with Balanchine at the New York City Ballet for the remaining dozen years of the elder man's life, even as he also continued to focus on other projects.

"He made this really extraordinary choice," said the dancer Mikhail Baryshnikov, who worked with both Robbins and Balanchine, "and he changed his life." Robbins, Baryshnikov felt, truly and wholeheartedly admired Balanchine, a "man who sometimes treated him roughly too, in front of a lot of people.

But he in many instances swallowed pride and learned from him." This decision to remain within the enveloping overcoat may have seemed to Jerry a symptom of his fears and anxieties. But from another perspective, it also signaled his own pragmatic strength.

The Cage

ONE OF THE ways Robbins differed most distinctly from Balanchine was in his sense of the relationship between men and women. For Balanchine, the woman was generally a treasured princess—sometimes a wistful, fragile, or victimized princess, sometimes a gorgeously triumphant one, but in any case someone to be nurtured, supported, or looked up to by the men around her. For Robbins, the interaction between the sexes was much more complicated. No doubt this stemmed from his own history, but it also may have come from an intuitive sense he had about the way American society was in the process of changing. In Balanchine's view, the old courtesies and old regulations still prevailed, especially in ballet, and it disturbed him when Jerry violated this inherited order. "Can you imagine?" he apparently barked about Robbins's 1970 ballet *In the Night*. "Old man stand, and beautiful woman in beautiful dress goes down on floor. Can you *imagine?!*"

In the Night was certainly not the first dance in which Robbins had questioned the standard roles assigned to male and female ballet dancers. Perhaps his most extreme exploration of the subject—a dance which in many ways remains as shocking now as when it first premiered—was one of the earliest, his 1951 work *The Cage*. It was a breakthrough work for him, and like a number of his most personal dances, it involved a measure of self-exposure. By the time he set to work on this piece, Jerry had become more than a little aware of his own confusion about sex and sexuality.

Among other things, he found he could not make a definite choice between men and women. Both sexes appealed to him as objects of desire, and both provided companions that mattered to him. His first homosexual experience, at least as he remembered it, took place around 1937 or 1938, when he had recently joined Gluck Sandor's troupe. As the designated youngster in the group, he apparently projected an aura of innocence, a noticeable need for protection and care. One night, when they were all out carousing, Jerry got very drunk, and in his semi-passed-out state he noticed that someone was holding his hand reassuringly. During the next company class, he asked a young dancer named Harry (which also happened to be the name of Robbins's father) whether he had been the one who held his hand. Harry responded that he had.

At that moment, as Jerry later put it, "a shocking thing happened. It was the realization that I was in love—and even more shocking—in love for the first time with a man." He was excited but also anxious, because "it made me unhappy to realize that I was queer." The two young men were inseparable for a while, but Harry, who was older and more experienced, kept the relationship from becoming fully sexual. When they finally kissed and embraced for the first time, Harry briefly fondled Jerry's crotch, but he could see from the boy's reaction that this was an unfamiliar move, so he suddenly pulled away, telling

Jerry that he was too young; and that, essentially, was the end of the relationship. (Years later, Jerry encountered Harry again and slept with him, but it turned out to be only a one-night stand: "It was good, but too late," Robbins recalled.)

Yet even as he learned this important fact about himself and his desires, Robbins was still torn. Part of him wanted to get married and have children—not only to please his parents (though that was certainly an element in his wish), but also because he was drawn to women, felt comfortable with them, and even enjoyed sex with them. The dancer Muriel Bentley, who had known him since 1938, claimed to have been his "first fuck," and by the summer of 1939 he had fallen in love with Albia Kavan, whom he had met at Tamiment. They broke up in the fall, though, during the Broadway run of *The Straw Hat Revue*, and at that point Jerry apparently acted flirtatiously enough with a fellow male cast-member to bring down his family's wrath. His sister, Sonia, showed up at the theater and told him that his behavior risked labeling him a homosexual, and that frightened him. Now twenty-one, he got back together with Albia for a while, but he also moved out of his family's house—whether because his parents had told him to leave or because he could at last afford his own apartment was never clear, though his later therapy-related reference to the "time of being ousted by family" at least hints at the former.

Not all his crushes took a sexual form. During the early 1940s he became very close to Horton Foote—his parting with "H.F." was the thing he noted most regretfully when he left New York on a Ballet Theatre tour in January of 1942—but nothing suggests that the relationship was physically intimate. The same could be said of his intense friendship with Tanaquil Le Clercq, which began at the end of that decade and lasted for the rest of both of their lives. That he felt a certain longing for this man and this woman is clear enough, but he was self-doubting enough (or perhaps self-aware enough) to realize that many of his longings would not materialize into full-blown affairs.

On the other hand, he *was* getting a lot of sex in those years, with people of both genders, and often the sexual encounters turned into something much more substantial. In 1947, for instance, he went out with and then became engaged to an attractive blond woman named Rose Tobias, whom he even introduced to his parents as his future wife. Rose adored Jerry ("He was beautifully proportioned, he had the most liquid brown eyes—I just loved to look at him"), and he certainly seemed to enjoy their sex life. But unbeknownst to her, he was still seeing Montgomery Clift, with whom he had been carrying on an affair since at least the previous winter. One night, when Rose was staying over at Jerry's apartment, Clift pounded loudly and drunkenly on the street door until Robbins finally let him in. Later Jerry explained the situation to Rose as well as he could, saying that he loved them both, that he wanted to be married even though he was ultimately more drawn to men, and that his psychiatrist had supported his wish to marry. But to Rose it all seemed too complicated and too strange, so she terminated the engagement.

By 1950, when he fled New York to escape the McCarthy Committee, part of what Robbins was fleeing was Ed Sullivan's threat to expose his homosexuality. Yet even at this point he was exchanging male partners for female ones and vice versa. In Paris he was joined by Nora Kaye, with whom he had been involved many years earlier, when they were both at Ballet Theatre. Nora's marriage to the musician Isaac Stern had recently broken up (she was ultimately to marry four times), and now she happily took up with Jerry again. He too seemed happy about it, writing in his journal in November of 1950:

> Nora is staying with me. I like it. I like the companionship
> & I like the sex. I guess yes it's like we have been married for

10 years & some of the excitement of a younger & more passionate kind of love (& not just sexually passionate) is miss-
ing. Nor do I feel a be-all-and-end-all feeling about it. Nor
do I at all think it a negative thing to say we get on well. It's
more than that, but that is plenty. Nor am I putting myself
on any test basis. What is, is, & what will be, will be & I no
longer expect perfection or disaster from myself. I'll indulge
I guess sometime elsewhere & otherwise sexually, I think—
but now this with Nora feels like home.

And it remained "home" long enough for Robbins and Kaye
to declare themselves officially engaged when they returned to
America. She too was taken to meet the parents, as Rose had
been, and in February of 1951 she joined Robbins at the New
York City Ballet, as if in anticipation of their planned April
wedding date. That the wedding was eventually delayed into
non-existence rather than outright canceled seemed, in the
end, to suit both of them.

Jerry was wrong, or perhaps just whistling in the dark,
when he asserted, "I no longer expect perfection or disaster
from myself," since that was a habit of mind that would follow him to his death. But he was absolutely right in predicting
that he would soon indulge "elsewhere & otherwise" sexually.
Only eight months later, in July of 1951, when he was again
in France, Robbins met Buzz Miller, the man with whom he
was to spend the next five years. The first thing Jerry told him
after their initial night together, according to Buzz, was that
he was engaged to Nora Kaye. "And I said, 'OK.' What could
I say? I'd never heard of Nora Kaye, and if he was engaged to
her, that was fine by me," Miller recalled many years later. "It
was never brought up again. He didn't indicate I was to leave,
so we went off to Finistère and had a wonderful time." They
didn't start living together right away—Buzz, significantly
younger than Jerry and nervous about what he had gotten
himself into, rushed back to New York alone, while Robbins

stayed on in Paris and had an interim affair with the composer Ned Rorem—but by early 1952 Jerome Robbins was sharing his Park Avenue apartment and his life with Buzz Miller.

By that time, though, he had already made *The Cage*. It seems odd that this dance should have emerged from his time with Nora Kaye, with its comfortable, familiar, unexciting but profoundly reassuring sex, because this unnerving dance presents exactly the opposite view of sexual relations between men and women. *The Cage* conjoins sex and self-realization, sex and terror, sex and triumph, sex and death. It is about rites of initiation, rites of community, and rites of exclusion. It elevates the female above the male, as Balanchine was wont to do, but it does so in a way that is explicitly frightening and disturbing. And it accomplishes all this while reflecting on, though also transforming, the styles and techniques of ballet.

The music for the piece—which is where Robbins started —was Stravinsky's twelve-minute *String Concerto in D*. Composed in 1946, it premiered in 1947, and Robbins had it on the flip side of a record that also contained Stravinsky's *Apollon Musagète*, to which Balanchine had choreographed his *Apollo* in 1928. To venture into Stravinsky for the first time was, for Robbins, to take a step onto turf that Balanchine had thus far reserved for himself, so it was a somewhat fraught project to begin with. Jerry listened to the music over and over, looking for some kind of dramatic thread that he could use in his dance. "And then I read a story about the Amazons," he said, and he began using that idea as the basis for his choreography. But when he looked at the steps and gestures he had come up with for the dance's first part, "I thought, 'This is terrible. . . .' Then I stumbled on information about insects and their prey," and after that, according to him, "it just went like a dream."

There is no cage in *The Cage*—no set of any kind, really, except a tangle of ropes (often described as a kind of spider's web) that rises from the stage and moves toward the ceiling at the start of the dance. The cast includes fourteen women and two men; when it begins, only women are onstage. Dressed in body-fitting leotards that are patterned in carapace-like shapes and colors, and wearing frizzy fright-wigs that make their heads look enormous, the dozen identical women are labeled the Group, while their similarly dressed leader is the Queen. To these thirteen are soon added a fourteenth, the Novice: a white-clad, wigless female who seems to emerge somehow from the Queen's body.

At first we cannot see the Novice's head—it is covered by a white veil, which also resembles a kind of sack—and she is pulled around blindly by the other women, as if she were a pupa or a puppet. (Something in her knock-kneed stance is slightly reminiscent of *Petrouchka*.) After her emergence she is left kneeling, or drooping, on the left-hand side of the stage while the others perform what seems to be a celebratory dance, including a solo by the Queen and a circle dance by the Group, all done with prancing, marching, turned-out steps that are markedly different from the Novice's turned-in style. Then they bring her from the side to the center, and all the others rush forward to quickly touch her body at every point with their insect-like hands, as if to groom her or perhaps infuse her with the group smell. The Queen then pulls her veil off, and we can see that she has very short hair and an expressionless face. Everyone else leaves the stage and she dances alone, stiff and insect-like, with strange twitches and pauses and cat-like arches of her back, but also using gestures that emphasize the length of her limbs, with upwardly extended arms or legs.

While we are still in the same musical realm—the percussive, march-like, yet also skitteringly intense first movement of the concerto—the solitary Novice is approached onstage by a male intruder. Her instinctive response is violent: she stomps him, puts his head between her knees, and breaks his neck with a twist of her legs. She pushes him over on his stomach with her toe, as if to make sure he is really dead. Then she does a kind of mini-victory-prance to the violins' percussive theme, making three passes back and forth, each time with an arm unfurling. She is joined by the other females, who carry the dead male body offstage (to be eaten, one presumes) and then come together for a group dance featuring the Novice front and center, paired with the Queen. At the end of this sequence, the young woman in white sits in a spotlit corner to the right while the rest of the Group and their Queen move offstage.

Now the Novice is joined by a second male intruder, but the music has changed to the more lyrical, adagio second movement, and something like a love duet ensues. This part looks more like normal ballet, with its legato movements and its intertwined couple, but the gestures are still faintly insect-like and occasionally agonistic—heads awkwardly thrown back, arms raised crookedly in sharp unison. There is a sense of tentativeness to both the music and the dance: things could go either way.

The way they do go, however, is the same as in her previous encounter, though the impulse to kill the male seems to be set off by the reappearance of the Group and not by the Novice's own instincts. The returning females collectively leap onto the intruder, pushing him backward as if to paralyze him; then they raise the Novice in their arms and lower her onto him. As the Group members perform a victory dance that simultaneously evokes a wasp hive and a showgirl chorus line, they allow (or perhaps force) the young Novice to deliver the coup de grace, and she duly breaks her lover's neck between her knees. Once he's been killed, she appears to have sex with him one final time, flattening herself over his supine body after she has kicked it over to the side of the stage. Is this a gesture of regret, or vengeance, or something that is entirely emotionless because it is not human?

By this time we have entered upon the concerto's third movement (which began at the end of the lovers' duet), and the most noticeable aspect of the music becomes its buzzing quality. The string instruments, which were sharply percussive in the first movement and melodically emotional in the second, have now been reduced to their most insect-like sound. As the music skirls and thrums to its wild conclusion, the members of the Group twirl individually in the background, while the spotlit Novice and Queen—their two spotlights melding into one—come together in the center of the stage in a revolving embrace. Then all fourteen women throw their arms up in the air and freeze on the final shrieking note.

It may sound a bit hokey when conveyed in words, but in performance this dance is both thrilling and unnerving. There is nothing platitudinous about it, and nothing cheap: it does not come across as being "about" sexual politics any more than it comes across as being "about" hive behavior. And this is because Robbins's sense of dance vocabulary, of gesture performed to music, is so subtle and original that the narrative and its means of presentation become completely fused. It is a dance that, among other things, uses ballet to comment on the insect-like qualities of ballet: the elongated, extended limbs of the dancers; the inhuman quality of the poses they are often forced to hold; the regimentation of the corps, and the relative superiority of the principals or soloists; above all, perhaps, the central role of the female. We are presented with all of Balanchine's beloved rules, here taken so literally that they are turned on their heads. At the same time, the dance offers us expressionism of the most intense sort, almost seeming to bypass technique in order to reach a moment of pure feeling. Whether that feeling is fear, or vengeful hatred, or disgust, or lurid attraction, or pure voyeurism, or something else entirely is a question that will depend partly on what the viewer brings to the dance.

For those who knew that the Novice role was danced at the premiere by Nora Kaye, the fiancée of the erstwhile gay choreographer, there must have been a tremendous temptation to read the piece biographically. At least one reviewer, John Martin, thought that the dance was "decadent in its concern with misogyny and its contempt for procreation," though he also praised it as a breakthrough work of genius. A little girl who had attended the premiere as Robbins's guest subsequently wrote him a letter saying that her mother had felt "you don't like women very much, but I told her you just don't like nasty women." The great critic Edwin Denby wryly commented that the movement quality of the oppressive Group was "literally that of the important Broadway people at parties and in offices."

Misogyny hardly seems a sufficient term to describe the fearsome, effective role of women in this dance. There is something both repellent and alluring about their manifest power: we can feel ourselves savagely expanding inside those roles even as we morally turn against them. Moreover, the fact that the victimized couple is a heterosexual one further complicates the interpretation. If the piece is to be read as social commentary, it needs to undergo a kind of Proustian inversion. That is, the true genders of the lovers—as in Proust—seem to have been disguised to fit the audience's sympathies, for in mid-century America wouldn't it be much more likely to be a *homosexual* couple that is persecuted by the controlling Group?

And if that reversal has been made surreptitiously, what else about the characterization needs to be reconsidered? Are these figures even human? Robbins, for one, seemed to want it both ways: he suggested that *The Cage* "is actually not more than the second act of *Giselle* in a contemporary visualization" while also insisting that it was really about bugs, not actual men and women. The choreographer also commented in a letter to Tanaquil Le Clercq that he was "very thrown by it opening night . . . it seemed no part of me," and he worried that perhaps the emotional meaning needed to be made more explicit. But whether the dance said anything about human love or even sex seemed a question he was unable to answer. Tanny, however, seemed certain: "I don't see *love* in The Cage at all—It isn't there, so why do you expect it?" she wrote him. "If she *loved* him which insects *don't* wouldn't she protect him? . . . I think it's fine the way it is."

One person who didn't appear to think *The Cage* was "fine the way it is" was the choreographer's mother. Invited to the premiere on June 14, 1951, Lena Robbins pointedly walked out halfway through the dance. She was clearly offended, but there is no firm evidence suggesting exactly why. Because she didn't like the explicit sexuality? Because she agreed with the charge of misogyny? Because she recognized herself in the powerful Queen? Any and all of these are possible.

Jerry's relationship with both his parents was complicated. He had felt their disapproval when he chose a career in dance instead of business, yet that feeling of rejection may have been stronger and more lasting in his own mind than in theirs; at any rate, they were so proud of his public success with *Fancy Free* and *On the Town* that in late 1944 they changed their last name from Rabinowitz to Robbins to match his. His feelings of anger and guilt toward both of them were manifest throughout his life, but his father tended to come in for more of the guilt, his mother for more of the anger. Harry was seen, in many ways, as the victim of Jerry's various betrayals—of traditional Judaism, of "normal" family life, of the sense of justice and fairness that his HUAC testimony had violated—whereas Lena was more often viewed as the oppressor. Linked at times with his intermittently disapproving older sister, she was the female force that functioned as his superego. "I couldn't put myself to the test as I knew I wouldn't pass it. Lena & Sonia won out," he wrote in his journal about a failed project that took place in 1976, more than twenty years after Lena Robbins had died.

Less than a month after the premiere of *The Cage*, when Jerry paid for both his parents to go to Israel while he was on tour there, he wrote to his friend Robert Fizdale, "Can't you just *imagine* the tons of guilt I'm shedding with this gesture!" And Lena's response to his gesture was suitably extravagant: "Dearest Sweetest Jerry," she thanked him. "It is needless to say how we feel. Emotions swept us away & we are still dazed." But running hot and cold had been her specialty throughout his life. It was what she gave him—practically forced on him— as much as what she took away that made him furious with both himself and her.

A little story he wrote in 1942 featured a son very much like himself confronting a mother very much like Lena. "I've got to take care of myself now Mom," the Jerry-character says. "I mean I want to help myself now instead of having you do things for me, you've got to see that." Over thirty years later, he would write in his journal (in the context of his lasting feelings of anger toward his mother), "I straighten my room as if someone I want to love will come into it & find it hospitable to be in. It will welcome them—or is it the kind of neatness I want to find in another. Perfection really rules me v/much." And at the very end he was still struggling to get away. Semi-comatose with exhaustion in the final months before his 1998 death, he at one point muttered in his sleep, "If my mother calls, tell her I'm not in."

To a certain extent, Robbins's attitude needs to be seen in the context of his extensive psychoanalysis. Especially in the 1940s and 1950s, American psychoanalysts were fond of attributing a man's homosexuality to an aggressive or overly controlling mother and a weak father; and though Jerry's first psychiatrist, a lesbian herself, was not necessarily a strong adherent of this theory, it clearly made a certain amount of sense to him.

But his homosexuality was by no means his only concern. It was his perfectionism, his anger, his constant self-doubt that really drove him mad, and these he attributed to his mother.

A single intense memory from his early childhood, set down in one of his notebook entries from 1972, supplied an example of what he viewed as the cause of his problems. It began with his mother's departure for work or some other appointment: "Mama Mama I was screaming—Don't go—please don't go & leave me—A housemaid—Annie—was holding me fiercely as I struggled to tear myself from her arms; I was crying. . . . The terror of separation & my love for my mother were so intense that my life & security depended on keeping her home—depended on her not forsaking me." Lena's response, as he recalled it, was "Cool. Still. Poised. As if her picture was to be taken." She didn't blow him a kiss or say a word to him, didn't "offer consolation or suggest comfort or assurance. She stood and gave me that look and left."

It doesn't matter, finally, how accurate Robbins's memories of his mother were. The cage doesn't have to be a real cage to hold its inhabitants captive. Mind-forged manacles can do as much as iron bars to keep people trapped in their old habits, their instinctive rites. And whether those patterns are generated by a species, a nation, a tribe, or an individual family, they will seem permanently unbreakable to the people who live under their control. No wonder *The Cage*—a dance in which no actual cage is visible or even gesturally implied—retains its power to disturb, to repel, and even to shock. The pressures and punishments it features are familiar to all of us, in some form or other. We may not all be forced to kill the thing we love, but something in us understands the temptation.

Afternoon of a Faun

Two YEARS AFTER the premiere of *The Cage*, Robbins made another dance about the relationship between men and women that took a completely opposite tack. If *The Cage* is a nightmare, *Afternoon of a Faun* is a dream: an entrancing, tender, beautiful yet somewhat unnerving dream which idealizes its male-and-female couple even as it also reduces them to the level of their actual, bodily, real-life selves.

In choosing Debussy's *Prélude à l'après-midi d'un faune* as his music, Robbins was once again venturing into terrain already staked out by a senior and much-respected choreographer. But in this case, at any rate, the competitor was long dead. Vaslav Nijinsky had famously choreographed his own *L'après-midi d'un Faune* in 1912, casting himself in the central faun role, complete with waxy pointed ears and silly tail, and ending the piece with a scandalous simulation of onanistic orgasm—a horizontal duet with a chiffon scarf. The dance was essentially a male solo with female chorus, featuring stylized, Greek-vase-like gestures on the part of both the elevated man and his attendant nymphs. The elaborate set and costumes, like the stiff arm gestures, all marked the piece as Mythic with a capital M. Borrowing the overheated quality of the Stéphane Mallarmé poem that inspired Debussy's composition, Nijinsky's revolutionary choreography duly shocked some audience members even as it delighted others.

By the time Robbins took it up, the music—originally perceived as an example of breakthrough modernism, a "tone poem" in which flutes carried the theme against a background of woodwinds, horns, strings, and harps—had become somewhat domesticated. In America, at any rate, it had already served as the background music for at least one Hollywood film (the 1949 *Portrait of Jennie*) and the theme-song for highbrow radio broadcasts. It was, in its own quiet way, the Pachelbel *Canon* of its time: lovely, evocative, but a bit sentimental and perhaps even at risk of turning into cliché. While superficially adding to its congenial familiarity, Robbins's use of this score for his modestly radical ballet actually gave it a new life of its own.

Nothing could be less like Nijinsky's heavily stylized and blatantly erotic dance than the gentle, moody creation that Robbins titled simply *Afternoon of a Faun*. Lasting a mere ten minutes, the dance comes across as both timeless and evanescent. The minute it's over you want to watch it again. It's not that you expect to see anything new, the second or third or tenth time, because the movement is so languorous and the choreography so clear that you can catch almost everything the first time through. It's more that you want to go back into that dream one more time—to be there again with those two enchanted beings who seem entirely encapsulated in their own world even as they also, somehow, reflect your own innermost wishes and desires.

As a single flute begins its song in the dark, the stage lighting gradually comes up to reveal a set that is essentially a ballet practice room contained in a translucent box. Waist-level
ballet barres line the walls of the box on three sides (the fourth
side, the one facing us, is open), and the door and window
slits cut into those walls lead outward to a blue-skyed, dark-
grounded space beyond. In the middle of the box, on the stage
floor, lies an indistinct sleeping body; when the gauzy scrim
lifts, we can discern a curled male figure, lying on his side with
his back to us. He rolls onto his back and extends one leg at a
ninety-degree angle toward the ceiling, briefly arches his upper
back off the floor, and then crosses his legs at the ankle. The
gestures could be either ballet movements or the stretches of a
waking man, and this confusion persists as he rises and moves
through a series of simple poses. He is at once a faun and a ballet dancer, dressed in black tights and black ballet shoes, but
bare-chested and sexy. When he looks out toward us, he seems
to be looking in a mirror at himself.

We see the woman before he does, for she enters through
the door-like slit in the wall behind him. She wears a kind of
sunsuit or very short tunic, her long legs revealed in pale tights,
with pale toeshoes on her feet. The sleeveless outfit empha-
sizes the grace of her arms and the length of her neck. Her
hair, which she wears loose and straight, is cropped at about
shoulder length and swings gently as she moves. At first, and
for what seems like a long time, she ignores the man: she too is
dancing for and looking at herself. Her smile is luminous, her
dance quietly joyous.

Even as he turns to look at her, she appears not to notice
him, instead going to one of the barres and performing a ballet-
class exercise. He comes around behind her and touches her
for the first time, encircling her with his arm—again, a gesture
that could be either the result of human longing or a standard
piece of ballet choreography. As he lifts her high in the air, she

still seems unaware of him, looking toward us the entire time (or rather, looking toward the mirror whose place we occupy). She notices him briefly when he turns her in his arms, but after allowing him to support her in several difficult positions, she steps away and does an equally difficult leg-lift on her own, as if to show that she is still a completely independent being. Even as he continues to lift and support her, the focus of both remains the mirror at the front, not each other.

But about a third of the way through the music—which for the most part remains unchanging in its stately pace, though with occasional quick runs on the flute or the harp—something alters. He strokes her hair and buries his face in it from the back. She arches slightly, turns toward him, and rises on pointe. Then they both lower themselves to the ground and look directly at each other, quickly looking away again toward us. When he lifts her again and sets her on his shoulder, she looks down at him, and after he lowers them both to the ground, holding her in his arms as if she were a child, she ends up sitting on his lap. Later still, when they are both looking out at us from a standing position, he cups her face in one hand and puts his other hand behind her head. Into the space that this creates between their bodies, she inserts one long arm and then the other, as if she were swimming out of a narrow hole in an underwater cave—and then she falls slowly forward and he catches her.

As the end of the dance approaches (though we don't necessarily realize that's what's happening, our first time through), the man and the woman sit on their haunches, bodies facing each other. She is looking out at us when he leans across and kisses her on the cheek. Still staring at the fourth-wall mirror, she touches her cheek lightly, just where he kissed it, in a wondering gesture; then she turns and looks directly into his eyes, as he does into hers. After this she rises and slowly backs off, disappearing through the same door by which she entered. The abandoned faun, or partnerless man, lies down again, first on his back, then on his stomach, and when the music ends, he is lying still, face-down. Whereas Nijinsky's final face-down faun had just executed an obviously orgasmic gesture, this one has simply lapsed into his dream, softly and gently.

Robbins's *Afternoon of a Faun* fits its music in a way that Nijinsky's never did, or rather, it brings out the floating, delicate, magical quality of the music rather than catering solely to its undertow of erotic fantasy (though the undertow is certainly there in the Robbins as well). This same floating quality, this utter absence of sharp or percussive gestures, is perhaps what lends the piece its tremendous feeling of innocence and tenderness. Even the self-engrossment of the mirror glances, rather than coming across as egotistical or arrogant, reflects an unsullied kind of self-fascination, as if a small child or some other unworldly creature were suddenly perceiving its own appearance for the first time, and wondering at it. And set against all the mirror-watching, those few passages of direct acknowledgment between the man and the woman are particularly moving. (Though, in a darker mood, one might argue that the whole dance is about the way this kind of literal narcissism obliterates the possibility of any lasting connection between these two characters, so that the moments of mutual recognition can only be fleeting. This too is part of the piece's gently indeterminate nature: the way it can float between these two opposing interpretations, depending in large part on who is dancing the roles.) In fact, the dance as a whole is profoundly touching in an almost inexplicable way—as if a few stylized gestures from a classical ballet class had been transformed into a piercing message about our own real and fantasy lives. Like the faun himself, we can scarcely credit what we have been through.

The dance was meant for Tanaquil Le Clercq, around whom Robbins explicitly shaped it, even borrowing some of her rehearsal-room gestures to put into it: her habit of lifting her hair off the back of her neck, for instance, or her way of stretching or sitting. "*Afternoon of a Faun* was choreographed on Tanny," Robbins later commented, going on to observe that "she had a terrific sexuality underneath, with the possibility of that which was much more interesting than the obviousness of it." Elsewhere he remarked, "Tanny had a quality about her that made you think of a young animal coming into its own, like a gauche young colt soon to become a graceful thoroughbred. There was a kind of aura about her." And when you watch her dance the part on film—for instance, in the 1955 recording that was made for Canadian television, with Jacques D'Amboise in the faun role—you can see exactly what Robbins meant. Other ballerinas since have performed the role well; the dance, which is one of Robbins's masterpieces, survives and even triumphs over cast changes. But nothing can equal the quality, both physical and emotional, that Tanaquil Le Clercq brought to it originally.

She had, from the very beginning, been the dancer who drew Jerry's glance. "Tanny Le Clercq made me cry when she fell backward at the end," he said of the 1948 *Symphony in C* performance that was his first exposure to Balanchine's company. "And I thought: Oh boy! I want to work with that company!" He quickly began to use this tall, leggy, coltishly graceful, subtly alluring dancer in his choreography, once he joined the New York City Ballet. And if the claim he made years later was a bit of an exaggeration—"All the ballets I ever did for the company, it was always for Tanny"—it nonetheless reflected how he felt.

Their personal connection was no less intense than their choreographic one, and each fed into the other. Though she chose Balanchine over him as a lover (or so he viewed it), their falling-out on this matter was brief, and they were soon chattering together at rehearsals as intimately as ever. "Balanchine once told me that to listen to a conversation between Jerry and Tanny was like listening to birds talk to each other," said Barbara Horgan, Balanchine's assistant. "Meaning that he didn't understand a word they said. They had a dialogue." And even after she took up with Balanchine, the intensity in their communications persisted. "Dearest Tanny, I got back to Rome yesterday, flew to American Express today, and found three letters and one post card from you. I kiss you on each cheek. I'd love to see you, tease you, have you make fun of me like you do," Jerry wrote to her from his European travels. He also wrote, "So many of the things I see, I picture you in them, on them, or looking at them too," and "Tanny, I love you so for just that quality, which really is very honest and always makes me blink at its directness and acuteness." And she responded in kind: "I hope you're happy. I'm glad that you exist. I wish that—Love, Tanny."

Like the two figures in *Afternoon of a Faun*, they recognized and understood the nature of the physical narcissism that they jointly shared, and it formed a part of their mutual attraction. This focus on their own bodies and each other's bodies, while natural in a dancer, took a heightened form in the connection between Robbins and Le Clercq, because for them the bodies were fully entangled with the minds. There was no separation, as their letters show, between seeing and feeling, between existence and communication, between directness of physical expression and directness of emotion. It was all one, in the choreography Robbins devised for Le Clercq, and if she was the instrument of his self-expression, she was also the shaper of his art.

That he understood something about her which her own husband missed was evident in the dances Robbins and Balanchine each made for her. Jerry loved her quiet strength, her youthful gaucheness, her animal quality of sensuality buried just beneath the surface, and he also loved her staunch, self-preserving wit. When he used her onstage, an intelligence seemed to emanate from every gesture—the same independent intelligence that, in a more antic form, characterized her spirited solo as a housebound but secretively rebellious wife in Lew Christensen's Rossini-inspired ballet, *Con Amore*. (Watching the few brief moments of that ballet which have been preserved on film, you almost feel that *Rossini* understood Le Clercq better than her husband did.) And certainly Robbins played to all those strengths in his 1953 *Afternoon of a Faun*, choreographed less than six months after her marriage to Balanchine, which took place at midnight on December 31, 1952. Even under these circumstances, Jerry seemed to be saying, she remained for him an independent figure, not a wife, and above all a woman, not a child. It was a distinction he insisted upon in at least one letter to her: "George is your ideal, good. But don't be a little girl about it and expect everyone else to be like him," he wrote.

For Balanchine, she always retained something of the "little girl," the skinny, smart teenager whom he had first noticed when she stood in the corridor of his ballet school, having been kicked out of her class for insubordination. In some of his choreography he even gave her the role of the talented but threatened child—as, for instance, in his March of Dimes benefit performance, in which Balanchine himself danced Polio and she danced the potential victim whom the March of Dimes saved at the end. More often she played the gloriously unobtainable woman, as all his leading ladies had done. What he valued about Le Clercq was her tallness, her thinness, her beauty, and her precision; clearly he also treasured her intense musicality, which made her able to interpret any score he chose for her. But what he also loved and used was her apparent vulnerability, something that was brought out, for instance, in *Symphony in C* (in her heart-stopping backward fall) and especially in *La Valse*, where he had her succumb to death itself. The girl who puts her long, shapely arms into the black gloves offered by the masculine figure of Death, swirls away with him to Ravel's volcanic music, and then collapses full-length on the stage cannot be a mortal wife to any man, for she is already taken by the king of the underworld.

"Balanchine needed the unattainable, had to be inspired by the unattainable," said the dancer Jacques D'Amboise. "But if he ever attained her, it wouldn't work." By 1956, when the New York City Ballet was planning its autumn tour of Europe, there were rumors that the Balanchine–Le Clercq marriage was already in trouble. Balanchine had been using the ballerina Allegra Kent more and more often in his new dances, and some people felt his romantic interest was now focused on her. As if in response to this neglect, Tanny turned once again toward Jerry. Robbins was no longer involved fulltime with the company—he was too busy putting on Broadway shows—but that summer she joined him for a weekend on Fire Island. (The relationship with Buzz Miller had recently ended, so Jerry had the summer rental house to himself.) Afterward, he wrote to her that he was still thinking of "the dunes and the night. . . . I can relive it all very easily." And she in turn wrote to him, as she set off for the European tour: "Darling—I'm going to miss you like crazy. . . . Can't possibly write, or say for that matter 'thank you' the way I feel it. I'm so bad with compliments, and so good with insults. . . . So bye—Be good—Have a nice summer—it seems so long till I see you, better perhaps, all the way round. All my love—T."

In addition to all the other anxieties of a long and exhausting foreign tour, there were the medical ones. Polio was rampant in the mid-1950s, and anyone who was likely to contract the disease was instructed to get a shot of the Salk vaccine. Jonas Salk's breakthrough discovery had first been announced in 1953, and it underwent testing for general use in 1954. "By the time we left for our tour to Europe," D'Amboise remembered, "the vaccine had come out, and we were all taking it. We're all lined up, a day or two before we took flight—the ballerinas, they're all standing ready to get their shot. . . . I had just got mine. And standing in line is Tanny, to get her shot. She got out of line, came over to me, and said, 'I'm gonna wait. I'm going to be miserable on a plane, I'll be even more miserable if I have a shot. I'll wait until I come back.'"

The other dancers noticed that Tanaquil Le Clercq was looking tired as the tour approached its end, and when they reached Copenhagen—the second-to-last stop on the agenda— Tanny herself felt as if she were coming down with the flu. So she rearranged her dance schedule that November night to eliminate the most challenging parts, performing only in the pieces that she felt she could manage with her heavy, aching limbs. She and Balanchine returned to their hotel room, and when she woke up in the morning she was paralyzed from the waist down. She was rushed to a hospital and put in an iron lung, which saved her life, though any further degree of recovery remained in doubt. It was, of course, polio.

The rest of the company went on to the last engagement, which was in Stockholm, and it was only on the train that they were told of Tanny's illness. Meanwhile, George Balanchine and Edith Le Clercq remained at her side. Tanny's French father had been pretty much absent from her life since a few years after her birth, but her mother more than compensated for it with her constant presence and supervision. Edith was one of those indomitable, privately ambitious American matrons who make the most memorable stage mothers. (One wonders, in fact, if Robbins—who knew her well and called her "Aunt Edith"—was borrowing from her personality when he later invented Mama Rose, the relentlessly pushy mother in Gypsy.) She had come on the European tour to keep her daughter company and enjoy a foreign vacation, and now she cast herself in the role of primary caretaker.

Balanchine, who may or may not have been on the verge of

leaving the healthy Tanny, was now completely in thrall to the sick one. A superstitious Russian (which is to say, a Russian), he felt horribly guilty at having cast her as a polio victim in the March of Dimes production, not to mention Death's victim in *La Valse*. But he was also an optimist, and he was convinced that she would someday walk and even dance again. For the moment, however, all he could do was wait.

Back in New York, to which the company had returned, Jerome Robbins volunteered to take over directing the New York City Ballet during the winter season so that Balanchine could remain with Le Clercq in Copenhagen. (This was a generous gesture on his part, since he was seriously occupied with Broadway shows at this time, both the 1956 *Bells Are Ringing* and the 1957 *West Side Story*. It also pained him emotionally to work with a company that now lacked his chief muse, and in fact Tanny's palpable absence was part of what kept him away from the New York City Ballet for years, in the period after Balanchine returned.) Before that, when he initially heard the polio news, Robbins had frantically called Lincoln Kirstein and offered to fly to Denmark if Tanny wanted him. "Be of good cheer Tanny. So much that happens doesn't make sense but you must know of my love for you and my deep concern of all that happens to you," he wrote to her in the hospital, and she slept with his letter on her pillow at night. After about a week she was able to scratch out a brief response with her left hand, the less damaged one: "Dear Jerry, I love you. XXX What a wonderful letter. I cried."

For as long as she remained in the Danish hospital, the two of them kept up their correspondence, and this in turn helped raise her spirits—though she alone, of the three waiting in the hospital room, was sure she would never walk again. "I keep asking: Why me? Why polio?" she said at one point, and then countered with "Oh, I always knew I had been so lucky so far, and that something would happen to George, Mother, or me. It just couldn't keep going on, all taking and no paying." But soon her sly wit began to emerge, even in these dire circumstances. At one point she sent Jerry a postcard of the famous statue in the Copenhagen harbor, Hans Christian Andersen's legless Little Mermaid, with a speech-bubble coming out of her mouth that said, "I am writing a letter to you." And in another letter she told Jerry, "In sitting up today, the nurses let go. I tried to sit up alone. What an odd feeling: you can't imagine what it's like. . . . I feel like a filet of sole trying to balance on its tail." She was also characteristically observant about Balanchine's role in her care: "George carried me to a chair. This is very nice as I could sit half hour now and maybe some tonight. I'm not 'chained' to my bed. George is *so* pleased. I would *almost* say he enjoys me this way. To have someone totally dependent on one seems to agree with some people."

When she finally returned to New York's Lenox Hill Hospital in March of 1957, Jerry was at last able to visit her. A series of photographs he took of her then show that despite her paleness, her wasted limbs, and her confinement to a wheelchair, she was still beautiful and even sexy, as she glanced sideways at him through her loose hair and occasionally gave him a small smile. That was in fact the point of the photos, which focused on her face and upper body alone: to show her that she was still beautiful, at least in his eyes.

By the summer she had been moved to a rehab hospital in Warm Springs, Georgia (the same place FDR had gone for *his* polio), and Balanchine was still assiduously attending her, going so far as to lift her up and hold her from behind and make her "walk" with her useless feet placed on his feet. He also prayed to his icons and religious relics, and asked that she do the same; she refused, though she sympathized with his feeling of helpless desperation. "It's almost better to have polio than to be near someone that has it," she wrote to Jerry.

Robbins's own approach was to drive down to Georgia in

a convertible and take her on a joyous picnic. Again, there are photos: the two of them seated in the sun on a blanket, he in a white shirt, she in checks, both smiling broadly at the camera; or Tanny sitting in the passenger seat of the open car, flirtatiously glancing back over her shoulder at him as he snaps the picture. "Dearest Jerry," she wrote him immediately after the visit, "the minute you left I did lots of laundry and cleaning of drawers, puffing my cigarette madly. You know, keep occupied so you won't think. I will think about the two days in the sun when I go to sleep, so I can dream them."

As the years went by and Tanny didn't get better, Balanchine eventually gave up and focused his attention back on his ballet company. Le Clercq longed to participate in the ballet world too—perhaps by helping to teach some of the younger students her roles—but according to Barbara Horgan, "Balanchine never wanted her to teach at the School of American Ballet. She would have loved to. He didn't want her near the school. It would have been an embarrassment for him. He didn't want the wheelchair in the school, and also their relationship—it would have brought it all back. Arthur Mitchell was the one."

Mitchell, one of the few African-American dancers in the company—and a sometime dance partner of Tanny's who had performed with her in *Western Symphony* the night before she fell ill—had recently left the New York City Ballet to form his own troupe, the Dance Theatre of Harlem. After consulting, interestingly, with both Balanchine and Jerry Robbins, he invited Tanaquil Le Clercq to become a teacher in his company. "My two leading dancers are really products of Tanny's," he said many years later. And she loved the work, which she managed to do from a wheelchair, with only one fully working arm and hand.

She also led an active social life, both before and after Balanchine left her for Suzanne Farrell (though that formulation makes it seem as if the leaving was all on Balanchine's side, whereas the decision was apparently mutual: both moved out of their shared apartment at the same time, without consulting each other). And Jerry was often if not always a part of that life. She gave an elaborate dinner party for one of his birthdays, where every course was named after a dance of his. He visited her at her country house in Weston, Connecticut, and she visited him at his summer places. He took her with him when he went to Spoleto in 1972 with his own dance group, Ballets: USA, and she enjoyed herself—though the ubiquitous stairs made it difficult to be a tourist, and at one point a companion on the trip, Randy Bourscheidt, actually dropped her on the stone steps. It was a terrible humiliation for the woman who had once been lifted onto a man's shoulder and brought down gently on his lap, all with the aid of her own strength and skill. Falling had become something she did helplessly, rather than in a willed and professional way. Yet she persisted with her life. "She was strong—her upper body was very strong," Bourscheidt noted. "That and her indomitable will were the reasons she could live alone." And through it all her beauty persisted even as she aged, her brown hair turning to silver as her high-cheekboned, sharp-chinned face remained very much the same. She was aware, too, that the dream of dancing would have come to an end later if not sooner. "It's one of those awful things," she once commented about the dancer's life, "that by the time you've arrived, you're already starting to diminish."

She and Jerry had periods of closeness and periods of falling away. "Tanny's relationship with Jerry Robbins was hot and cold. She found him maddening, because it was always what suited him. Sometimes he was in her life and then he was not in her life," said Barbara Horgan. After Balanchine's death in 1983, when Le Clercq inherited the rights to Balanchine's *Nutcracker*, they had a serious disagreement over the credits for the children's dance that Robbins had helped choreograph. But this was resolved, and by the time death was nearing for the two of them (they died two years apart, he in 1998 and she in 2000), they were friends again. When he lay in the hospital during his final illness, she spoke to him briefly on the phone. "I love you," she said, and he answered, "I love you."

Before that, he had dreamed more than once about Tanny—important dreams that affected him powerfully. In 1976, he wrote down a dream in which she had been able, at long last, to walk. "Isn't it terrific, she said—I cried so—& then she wanted to know the limits of her recovery—piqueted forward to peek into a hospital room—& in that gesture I saw all the immense talent she had for dancing." And in the spring of 1994, when he himself was seventy-five years old, he had a piercingly intense dream that was set in an outdoor flower market in Paris. As he noted in his journal, it began with a voice calling him:

> Jerry. Said simply & quietly. I turned back. There stood Tanny. Tall, slim, a small straw hat perched on her head—a quiet look on her face—framed within all the wispy trailing plants. She held a small parasol over her head, an early spring or late fall coat lightly draped over her shoulders.
> I looked at her. Her regard was all acceptance—forgiveness. I said Tanny—& walked over to her, put my arms around her, & kissed her on the lips. She was young (& older), slim, sad, clear eyed, and oh so touching. I looked at her again . . . I kissed her fervently again it was home.

For Jerome Robbins, Tanaquil Le Clercq was both a real person with her own real life and an imagined entity he had absorbed within himself—a source of inspiration, a source of self-forgiveness. She was a body that was separate from his, with its own beautiful nature, its own set of incomparable abilities; and she was also a mind, or let us say a soul, that he felt particularly able to commune with.

That is the duality he presents in *Afternoon of a Faun*, and it is partly why the dance has remained so powerfully moving in all the decades that have passed since he first made it for her. The Mallarmé poem that lies behind the piece speaks of "the soul / Weighed down by the body, wordless, struck dumb"—a phrase which might almost seem to forecast the fate that overtook Tanny, the illness that smothered her eloquent gestures. But the sense of the dance is not that, for in Robbins's hands the soul is *not* weighed down by the body, but is given expression through it, made alive through it. There is no separation in this dance between soul and body, allegory and substance, dream and reality. The nymph is also an actual ballerina; the dream that the faun can't be sure he had is something we ourselves saw in the flesh. We are there in this couple's presence, as they are there in ours, and for once the cold mirror that is usually capable only of giving back a deceptive veneer has been turned into something warm and responsive and affirming: that is, us. We, the witnesses who are also the reflections of this two-person tale, are the thing that gives it endless life; and, at least for the duration of the dance, it feels as if it is returning the favor.

West Side Story

HE HAD BEEN working on the idea, in some form or other, for years. As far back as 1947, when his then-lover, Montgomery Clift, was taking the part of Romeo in a scene from Shakespeare's play, Monty asked Jerry for his advice on how to play the role, and Jerry responded that he should think of it as if he were an Irish Catholic kid from the neighborhood who had fallen in love with a Jewish girl: what would be the allure, what would be the risks, and who would get angry about it? Or perhaps Robbins's ideas about restaging the play came to him even earlier, when he was dancing the part of Benvolio in Antony Tudor's ballet version of *Romeo and Juliet* in 1943.

By the beginning of 1949, at any rate, he had confided his thoughts to his frequent musical collaborator, Leonard Bernstein. "Jerry R. called today with a noble idea: a modern version of Romeo and Juliet set in the slums at the coincidence of the Easter-Passover celebrations," Bernstein noted in a January 6 entry in his journal. "Feelings run high between Jews and Catholics. Former: Capulets. Latter: Montagues. Juliet is Jewish. Friar Lawrence is the neighborhood druggist. Street brawls, double deaths—it all fits. . . . Jerry suggests Arthur Laurents for the book." Laurents was indeed brought in, and the rough outline of a plot and dialogue for a production that had various working titles—*Gang Bang, East Side Story, Gangway, Romeo*—was sketched out by the three of them within a year. Whether this would be an opera (as Bernstein hoped) or a musical comedy (as Laurents expected) was still an open question at that point. Robbins, from the beginning, seems to have imagined a middle ground. "I didn't like the idea that we had to separate ourselves in two halves, one the commercial half and one the classical half, the long-hair half," as he later expressed it. "Why can't we put them together . . . and do our best work in the popular theater?"

It was a moot question, at that point, because the three principals soon became too busy with their own pursuits—Laurents with screenwriting, Bernstein with conducting and composing, Robbins with a mix of Broadway and ballet assignments—to take the idea any further. But when gang violence became front-page news in the mid-1950s, with movies like *The Wild One* and *Rebel Without a Cause* bringing motorcycle riders and juvenile delinquents to the big screen, the idea once again seemed highly topical. The three creators reunited to work on the project, and Laurents persuaded Robbins to convert the Jews and Catholics into opposing teenage gangs. The exact nature of those gangs, along with the musical rhythms that would underlie their characters, suddenly took shape in Bernstein's mind in August of 1955, when he and Arthur Laurents were sitting by the pool at the Beverly Hills Hotel. It was a newspaper article about Chicano gangs in Los Angeles, Lenny wrote in his journal, which had caught his eye and given him the form he needed: "I hear rhythms and pulses, and—most of all—I can sort of feel the form."

By the winter of 1955–56, the *Romeo and Juliet* production—now renamed *West Side Story*, after the Puerto Rican gangs on the West Side of Manhattan—had acquired a crucial new team member, Stephen Sondheim, who was brought in to help Bernstein with the lyrics. Sondheim, a recent Williams College graduate introduced by Arthur Laurents, was a promising young composer who had thus far done nothing on Broadway, but after working with him briefly, Lenny called him "a find." This was no understatement. If *West Side Story* turned out to have better songs than any other musical Bernstein wrote or Robbins directed, with not a single dud in the bunch, that was at least partly thanks to the verbal and musical talents of this prodigiously gifted lyricist. (Bernstein acknowledged as much when he kindly gave up his "Lyrics by" co-credit during the out-of-town tryouts so that Sondheim, who had been ignored by the early reviewers, would get full credit.)

The younger man, too, was learning a great deal from the process, and he remained eternally grateful for the opportunity to collaborate with Jerome Robbins. "Jerry is the only genius I've ever met, my definition of genius being endless invention," Sondheim commented years later, after his own fame had ballooned to Robbins-level proportions. Noting that Jerry was "a good collaborator except when you wanted to argue a point," Sondheim went on: "Difficult as he was to work with, and he could be really mean—awful man—I would work with him again any time. The end product was worth it."

Jerry's meanness emerged in all sorts of ways on this project. The performers, as always, came in for nightmarish treatment. The auditions were high-anxiety stress tests meant to lay bare their innermost qualities; once selected, they then had to abide by all of Robbins's harsh rules separating Jets from Sharks, both onstage and off. The physical demands on the dancer-singer-actors were extraordinary, the psychological pressures even more so. Even when dealing with his evident favorites, Jerry relied on gentle mockery to make his point. Addressing Chita Rivera, who played the key role of Anita in the stage version, he once said, "Chita. Don't dance to the window. Walk to the window, run to the window, crawl—but just be a person."

Nor was he kinder to his chief collaborators. He and Arthur Laurents squabbled constantly over the basic script (said to be the shortest book ever for a Broadway show, because Robbins ended up expressing everything through dance and song). He fought with Laurents over specific characterizations, nixing his original Anita, for instance. "You're way off the track with the whole character of Anita," he wrote him when they were on opposite coasts, calling her "a terrible cliché" and adding: "If she's 'an-older-girl-kicked-by-love-before-experiencing-the-worst' (and I'm quoting you) she's much too experienced for the gang, or else is sick, sick, sick to be so attached emotionally and sexually to a younger boy of a teen age gang. I can't put the above strongly enough and at the risk of offending you, Arthur, forget Anita . . . "

Even Leonard Bernstein, his longtime collaborator, was terrified of Jerry's sharp tongue, and with good reason. Though they continued at times to work in their old way, with Jerry's hands resting on Lenny's shoulders as they played out ideas on the piano, there were also numerous spats about how the music should go, with Jerry insisting on having things his way. A particularly humiliating moment for Lenny took place during the Washington, D.C., dress rehearsal. "Jerry and Lenny had argued over the orchestration of 'Somewhere,'" Stephen Sondheim recalled. "So when the orchestra was playing it in the pit, Jerry just ignored Lenny, went down to the pit, and stopped the rehearsal, and dictated changes in the music to the conductor, right there in front of Lenny." (Among the other things he was heard to say was "Take that Hollywood shit out!") Sondheim found the whole episode "really shocking. And Lenny, instead of confronting him, left the theater," temporarily hiding himself away in a bar across the street.

Though Robbins didn't argue publicly with his set designer, Oliver Smith, or his lighting designer, Jean Rosenthal, they too came in for animosity—from backers and producers who had never seen such a strange, fluid, movie-style set, or who didn't understand the importance of lighting. The show, in fact, lost its original producers in the course of its development, which was another factor that explained its slow evolution. And Jerry did not help matters when, rather late in the day, he threatened to withdraw as choreographer and stay on only as director. Hal Prince, who had by then come on as co-producer with his partner Robert E. Griffiths, countered that threat by offering a longer-than-usual rehearsal period and allowing Jerry to hire a co-choreographer, Peter Gennaro (though the contract Robbins negotiated with Gennaro kept him on a very tight leash, giving Jerry "any and all rights in and to any and all choreographic material created or suggested by you . . . as fully as if your said choreographic material and conceptions had been originally created or suggested by me").

Robbins was, of course, always a bear to work with, as he himself knew. "I know I'm difficult. I know I am going to hurt your feelings. But that's the way I am," he said at an early meeting of the *West Side Story* cast. And if his behavior on this show was worse than usual, that may have been due in part to the disruptions his personal life was undergoing during the entire period of its gestation. In April of 1955, his mother died of breast cancer, with Jerry at her hospital bedside—and though the occasion allowed him to reconcile at long last with his sister, Sonia, it still caused him profound distress. By 1956, his five-year relationship with Buzz Miller had fallen apart, with nothing of equal substance arriving to take its place. And toward the end of that same year, Tanny Le Clercq fell ill with polio.

But if those years were difficult for Jerry emotionally, they also represented a triumph professionally, and this too may have figured into his behavior on *West Side Story*. Whereas Bernstein was coming off the relative failure of his poorly reviewed *Candide*, which opened briefly on Broadway in December of 1956 but closed less than three months later, Robbins had not one but two recent successes under his belt: *The King and I*, the first musical-turned-movie he was ever hired to choreograph (*On the Town* having been handed over to others); and *Peter Pan*, his first venture into conceiving, choreographing, and directing a whole show. By 1957, when rehearsals for *West Side Story* began, *Peter Pan* had not only been a great hit during its limited run on Broadway; it had also become, starting in 1955, a near-annual television broadcast that was to shape the imaginations of a whole generation of American children. No wonder Robbins had the conviction that he, and he alone, was the right person to make the decisions about *West Side Story*. He had just accomplished something equally adventurous, though perhaps on a somewhat smaller canvas, in his innovative production based on J. M. Barrie's play.

From its first appearance on the London stage in 1904, followed by its gradual evolution as a staple of the British "panto" tradition, *Peter Pan* had a long history as a Christmas treat for children. As recently as 1953, moreover, Disney had brought out its own *Peter Pan* as an animated film, thereby giving it the official imprimatur as a sentimental cliché. But Robbins, with his real sense of connection to childhood—both his own and that of the children he had worked with onstage—figured he could do something new with the material. As he said, "I thought I could find a way of doing it less cutely and more robustly."

The song-and-dance music he commissioned from Moose Charlap and Jule Styne cannot compare with Bernstein's score for *West Side Story*, nor do the lyrics by Carolyn Leigh and Comden & Green approach the cleverness of Sondheim's. But Robbins's *Peter Pan* is nonetheless an amazing achievement, something that transcends its genre as surely as Peter's flying transcends gravity. The flying, which Robbins borrowed from the traditional panto version, is one of the memorable events for anyone watching the show, whether in the theater (where Peter soared out over the heads of the closest audience members) or on television (where the backdrop window of the Darling children's nursery flew open to reveal a starry sky from which the green-clad figure first zoomed into the room). It is a sight that never fails to lift the heart, appealing as it does to something that is at the root of our feelings about dance: that dance *is* flight, or as close as we will ever get to it. "I like *Peter Pan* better than anything in the world," the choreographer Mark Morris has said. "I'm talking about the TV show— the best thing I've ever seen in my life. It wasn't just associated with my childhood on black-and-white TV. It's actually magic. You can see the wires, and it doesn't matter. The characters, the unbelievable staging—the choreography is just miraculously good, and terribly, terribly moving."

Clever things abound in the show, beginning with the fact that the titular boy is actually played by a woman, the graceful and accomplished Mary Martin. This (again, traditional) casting— especially in the duet "Mysterious Lady," where Martin employs her famed coloratura to enchant Captain Hook—allows Robbins to play with the girl-disguised-as-a-boy-disguised-as-a-girl gimmick that derives from, among others, Shakespeare and Handel. And, as in Shakespeare and Handel, Robbins's use of this practice alerts us to the fact that fantastical, incredible stage conventions, the kind of thing we routinely write off with the phrase "suspension of disbelief," are going to bring us real emotional truths. Consider Tinkerbell, who is not even a live person, but a combination of flickering lights and high-pitched bells in whom we are nonetheless expected to believe—literally so, in the near-death scene after Tink has drunk the poison that was meant for Peter. "Your voice is so low I can scarcely hear what you're saying," Peter tells her, and then interprets, as he always does: "You're saying, you could get well again if children believed in fairies?" And then Peter turns and speaks directly to the fourth-wall audience in the theater and in television land: "Do you believe? If you believe, wherever you are, clap your hands and she'll hear you. Clap . . . clap . . . " One would need to have the heart of Oscar Wilde to hear these lines without weeping.

Just as Martin, through her passionate conviction, makes us believe in Tinkerbell's separate existence, she also makes us feel that she is really one of the Lost Boys—perhaps a bit older and more experienced and more assertive than the rest of them, but a child nonetheless. In the scenes where they build Wendy's house or battle the pirates together, she is just another one of the children, or so Robbins's direction suggests. And if Martin is a woman and a boy, a child and an adult, then the Indians are simultaneously foes and friends, harmless "play" Indians of the sort that any 1950s child would be familiar with from summer camp and playground games. The casting of blond, ponytailed Sondra Lee in the role of Tiger Lily, not to mention the inclusion of lyrics like "Ugga-wugga-meatball," suggests as much. If this is offensive to a modern ear, it is less so than the earnest Siameserie of *The King and I*, which takes itself much more seriously. To the social critic who objects that these are not real Indians, one might reasonably say, "And are these real pirates?"

Nothing in the show, in fact, survives childhood as wonderfully as Captain Hook, who, as embodied in Cyril Ritchard, is surely one of the great stage villains of all time. The thrill lies not just in his overt theatricality (his curly wig, his Restoration-comedy beauty mark, his laces and velvets), and not just in his graceful performance (though his little skips, waltzes, and kicks are indeed delightful), but in a kind of communion between Hook and the audience, signaled by the fact that he alone is awarded intense close-ups in the filmed-for-TV version. With Hook and his fellow pirates, it is not just the case that, as Orwell wrote of the Murdstones in *David Copperfield*, they "dwindle from gigantic figures of doom into semi-comic monsters" as we grow older and encounter them again. It is more that, *even as a child*, one senses the duality of Captain Hook—the way he is both a thing in itself and our projection of that thing, a feared monster and a beloved, hilarious monster, all at once.

For *West Side Story*, Robbins took another tack entirely. He did not want us to think about staginess, or theatricality, or performances within performances. He wanted the whole thing to seem incredibly real to us—as real as it was to him, as real as he had made it for the actors suffering through their roles. He wanted the mesh between the imagined, music-inspired, dance-filled world and the actual, gritty, streetwise world to be seamless. And for this reason, the 1961 movie version of the show, which Robbins helped direct (until he was summarily fired), may be the truest form ever taken by this particular musical. It is, at any rate, the only form now available to us, since all restagings done after Robbins's death are just that—redoings of his idea, and even of his specific choreography—whereas this version alone shows the enduring mark of his mind, his hand, his ear, and his eye.

Possibly no film has ever had a better opening. The first thing we hear is a brief sound of whistling in the dark. Then the Bernstein music starts up, and we are staring at a still screen that looks something like a player-piano score, with its vertical lines of different lengths and spacings—a screen that gradually changes color, from yellow to red to purple to blue to orange to green, as various songs from the musical are played in a medley.

After five minutes of this, the camera pulls back slightly, revealing the words "WEST SIDE STORY." Then the lines of the player-piano morph into the skyscrapers of Manhattan, as seen from above, and the picture starts to move: we are flying over the city, above recognizable and unrecognizable landmarks, and the soundtrack has turned from music to something indifferentiably urban, a mixture of distant traffic noise, whistling, and bongo drums.

As the music hesitantly starts up again (accompanied by a clicking sound that we don't necessarily recognize), we zoom in on a concrete playground where teenage boys are lounging against a cyclone fence. These Jets—though we don't yet know they call themselves the Jets—are snapping their fingers in unison, which explains the source of that background noise. Now the music begins to build and they start to move in time with it, walking, tossing a ball, leaping upward to make a basket, tilting their heads, flexing their shoulders. It is natural movement and dance movement all at once; the two have become essentially the same thing. And now, as they start to move down the street together, more dance moves enter in, including some leg lifts in unison and more extreme skips and leaps. But because the transition has been so gradual, this too seems an outgrowth of their natural movement, not artificial or stagy at all. (If we are observing this scene very carefully, we might also notice that the camera that shows us all these moves is located quite low, often shooting from beneath the level of the boys themselves. Robbins apparently had trenches dug in the street to produce these lower camera angles: he wanted the dancers to seem raised up high, as they had been on the stage, but also threateningly imposing, with their added height exacerbating the sense of movie characters' larger-than-life presence.)

Eventually these white boys run into their first Shark, Bernardo—though, just as we don't yet know they are Jets, we don't know he is a Shark, and nor do we know that he is the brother of our heroine, Maria, and the leader of the Puerto Rican gang. But we can sense from the menacing gestures on both sides that he's an enemy, an antagonist. After they leave him alone, he is joined by two other Sharks—and at this point we begin to notice the beautiful colors the camera is picking up as it lingers on the dark skins of these boys, their red or purple shirts against the dark-red of the brick walls and the bright graffiti. Now the camera follows the three Sharks as they dance down the street, until they encounter two paler Jets and follow them with catcalls like "Hey, Jet-boy!" This is the only speech we've heard thus far, and it is exceedingly brief, almost a punctuation of the music.

Back at the basketball court, the Sharks confront the Jets, and the music comes to a dead stop. The Jets yell things like "Beat it!" and "Chico!" (still hardly what you would call movie dialogue), and the Sharks leave. Then the music starts up again and the Jets play basketball—choreographed basketball, exactly on the beat, but with a real ball. (One is reminded of the real gum wrappers the sailors threw away in *Fancy Free*: it may be dance, but it borrows the props of real life). From the game we move into a two-man fight between one Shark and one Jet, and then a rout in which a whole gang of Sharks chases after and captures the most childlike of the Jets, Baby John, who leaps into the air and is caught by them. The choreographed fighting never lets go of the aura of *real* fighting, so that the thrill of the danced performance also combines with a constant and growing sense of menace—for instance, when the boys rush down the street toward us, their fingers snapping in unison. By the time the cops enter the scene to break up the fight, which is the moment when real dialogue starts, we are fifteen minutes into the movie, and we are immersed in a world where dance and life, staging and reality, have become one and the same. It's unlike anything else ever captured on film, and it never grows old, however many times you've seen it and however many decades have passed since it was made.

The fluidity of this opening sequence carries into the rest of the movie, so that the moments when the characters break into song are not jarringly announced by portentous pauses, as they are in most other musicals, but instead seem to arise organically out of the moment and the music. "When You're a Jet" begins with a shouted/spoken line on the part of the gang's leader, Riff, and then morphs into a full song and dance. "Officer Krupke" emerges from a scene in which the gang members taunt the buffoonish cops who "believe everything about us JDs." Maria tries on hats in the mirror of the bridal shop, a moment that leads naturally into her "I Feel Pretty." "Cool" begins with angry speech, then reintroduces the finger-snapping rhythm and eventually, as the music rises, broadens into expansive gesture and finally dance. The incomparable "I Like to Be in America"—perhaps the greatest dance sequence in the movie, with the cleverest lyrics and the catchiest tune—springs directly from a spat Anita has just had with her boyfriend, Bernardo, about his treatment of his sister. And so on, for all the great songs in the movie. There is not a bad one in the bunch; even the passages that are not carried by lyrics or character (as, for instance, in Tony's solo "Maria," sung as he walks alone down the street) are carried by the gorgeous music.

Tony is, alas, the big problem in the movie, because the actor selected to play him, Richard Beymer, is like an empty hole in the middle of the screen. He is not particularly goodlooking (especially compared to the enchanting George Chakiris, who plays Bernardo, his opposite number among the Puerto Ricans); he can't sing at all (both his and Natalie Wood's songs were dubbed in by professional singers); and, unlike Natalie Wood, he can't even move gracefully. But somehow this doesn't ruin the film, in large part because Natalie Wood is so luminous, so full of conviction, and so persuasive in her role that she carries the love scenes involving the two of them. Robbins has made this into *her* story, above all, and he signals this by having the final tragedy rest with her. In letting his Juliet survive at the end, he actually manages to create more pathos than he would have by allowing her to die.

The role of the music cannot be overstated, but nor can the role of silence. In those last few moments of the movie—just as he did in the stage play—Robbins silenced the background orchestra and left the emotion to the voices themselves. "I didn't believe hard enough," says the dying Tony to Maria, to which she responds, "Loving is enough." "Not here," says Tony, "they won't let us be." "Then we'll get away," she answers him, and begins singing softly to him, a capella: "Hold my hand and we're halfway there. Hold my hand and I'll take you there. Somehow. Someday. Some—" Her last word cuts off into silence, and only then does the music, in a very reduced and quiet form, carry her melodic line onward. The cops show up with their flashing red lights, but she angrily tells them, "Don't you touch him!" She kisses Tony's dead lips ("Te adoro, Anton," she murmurs, echoing a line from their pretend-wedding scene), and then four members of the teenage gangs—two Sharks, two Jets—lift his body and carry him out.

That final scene takes place at night, as does much of the rest of the film, and the colors and lighting, the intense reds and blues against the shadows, have by this time become almost as important a signature as the movie's music and dance. Many of the film's shots are as visually striking as an Alex Webb photo of Mexico or Cuba, with the screen's rectangle divided up vertically and horizontally into color and shadow, while the people show up as silhouettes or as faces displayed against red-brick, graffiti-filled walls, all lit by the kind of intense urban lighting (neon, car headlights, streetlamps, indoor-outdoor contrasts) that picks out color in a special way.

Watching the movie decades after it was made, you may begin to find its visual quality familiar in an ex post facto way. It is very similar, for instance, to the look of *Do the Right Thing*, Spike Lee's breakthrough film. Surprising as this connection may seem, it is a real one, for when asked on Twitter whether he had ever watched any movie more than twenty times, Lee put *West Side Story* at the top of his list. Arguments about cultural appropriation seem pointless in this context, for the visual artist takes what he needs, and in the case of both Robbins and Lee, what they needed was a kind of urban romantic realism, neither completely of this world nor totally apart from it. The color and life that Robbins gave to his Puerto Rican characters (for it is they, and not the Jets, who dominate the film visually) turn out to be equally suitable for Spike Lee's African-American and Italian-American characters.

And the fact that Robbins's are not "real" Puerto Ricans may also be beside the point. Mark Morris recalled that when he was working on the musical *Capeman*, "the cast were like, you know, 'Fuck *West Side Story*. It's the opposite of Puerto Rican. It's very touristy.'" But for him, both as a choreographer and as a lover of movies, that hardly mattered. "It is great in every way," he said of Robbins's film. "Of course! I'm sorry, that's the best movie ever made. I cry at the credits. It's incredible, I love it, it's perfect. I accept it entirely. I don't have any reservation about that movie. Except," he added, "it's phony Puerto Rican."

Perhaps. But unlike the Siamese of *The King and I* or the Indians of *Peter Pan*, the Puerto Rican characters come across as in many ways the heroes of *West Side Story*. Even though they are played mainly by non-Hispanic actors, something of the culture's vitality—whether in Bernstein's Latin-influenced music, or the vivacity of the speech patterns they are assigned, or the intensity of the colors they wear—emerges admirably intact. Certainly the source of the dance style was, for Robbins, at least partially Puerto Rican. "They do dances I've never seen before," he reported to Tanaquil Le Clercq about his visit to a high-school dance in Spanish Harlem, "evolving their own style and approach. In once dance, after starting with your partner for about 2 bars, you leave and separate and never touch or make contact again for the whole rest of the dance"—a description that may remind you, if you have seen it, of *West Side Story*'s dance at the gym. Ethnicity may be stylized here, but it is stylized in favor of the Puerto Ricans (who were originally Jews, remember, in Robbins's first conception: the outsider Capulets set against the more mainstream Montagues). And there is at least one other foreign influence here as well. Bernardo himself seems to comment obliquely on his affinity with a previous Robbins character, the charismatic King of Siam, when he exits one scene by saying to the assembled ladies, "Etcetera etcetera etcetera"—the King's most characteristic line from *The King and I*. In mocking his resemblance to the faux-Eastern Yul Brynner, George Chakiris is both pointing out the potential similarity and emphasizing the difference.

A great part of the difference lies in the fact that *West Side Story* is actually *about* racism in a way that *The King and I* and *Peter Pan* are not. The cops' vicious attitude toward the "PRs," as they call them, is central to the plot and dialogue, and it is almost shocking, still, to hear the lieutenant say to the Sharks assembled in Doc's drugstore: "So what if they do turn this whole town into a stinking pigsty? . . . Oh, I know, it's a free country. But I got a badge. What do you got? Beat it!" And this attitude in turn strengthens the power behind Maria's words at the end, when she says to the assembled onlookers, *including* the cops: "All of you—you all killed him. And my brother. And Riff." It was not just a matter of feuding clans, as in the original *Romeo and Juliet*. It was an unfairly weighted battle between two dif-

ferently treated ethnicities, and Robbins's sympathies clearly
lay with his Juliet.

The positive reactions to the staged version of *West Side
Story* came early and strongly. When the cast performed the
whole piece informally in a tryout before their invited peers,
the intensity of the audience reaction amazed them. "The first
time we did it for the gypsy run-through," said Chita Rivera,
"we didn't know what we had." But the outpouring of tears and
applause gave them a solid hint. "I tell you, this show may yet
be worth all the agony," Bernstein wrote to his wife after that
performance. And when at last it was reviewed by the critics—
first during the out-of-town previews in Washington, D.C.,
and then after the September 26, 1957, Broadway premiere—
West Side Story became an instant hit. Even before the critics
weighed in, the audiences had made their feelings clear, with
roaring applause after the first act and stunned silence (followed by roaring applause) at the end.

A year later, on September 14, 1958, the eternally creepy
Ed Sullivan—now a Robbins booster, as a result of Jerry's 1953
HUAC testimony—broadcast one of the musical's dance numbers on his television show. Calling *West Side Story* "one of the
greatest musicals of all time" and going out of his way to note
that "the conception by Jerome Robbins was quite original,"
Sullivan introduced "this magnificent ballet, which is called
'Cool.'" After the dancers from the stage show had performed
the somewhat modified-for-TV number, Sullivan turned to
his TV viewers and said, "I want you to meet Jerome Robbins
later. He's out in our audience," adding with a cagily vague
pronoun, "You know, they've contributed so much, so vastly to
the whole level of Broadway entertainment." Eventually he did
call on Jerry to make himself known: "Jerry Robbins, wherever
you are, stand up, won't you please? Here he is, here's this brilliant young choreographic genius and director." Smiling shyly,

Jerry stood up briefly but said nothing. Aged forty now, he was no longer the glossy young dancer who had performed in *Fancy Free*. He had begun to bald severely, though the hair that remained was black, and he was still clean-shaven and notably svelte. For those who later came to know the iconic image of the white-bearded, completely bald, authoritative Jerome Robbins, this surprisingly innocent-looking person would have appeared to be a figure in transition.

A similarly shy and ageless figure got up to accept the Academy Award for Best Director in April of 1962, when the 1961 film won an astonishing ten awards at the annual Oscar ceremony. Robbins had to share his directing award with Robert Wise, the co-director who had essentially gotten him fired from *West Side Story* when it was running overtime and overbudget. (Wise had also refused to listen to Jerry's notes about the dance at the gym, the only dance sequence that hadn't been filmed by the time Robbins was dismissed; and the result is that even now, watching the movie, you can detect how unclear and messy and disappointingly *unthreatening* this number is, compared to what it would have been in Jerry's hands. Robbins was a master at suggesting the shifting ownership of dance space by competing gangs or clans: he had done it with pirates, Lost Boys, and Indians in *Peter Pan*, and he was to do it even more forcefully with Jews and Cossacks in a crucial number from *Fiddler on the Roof*. But because of this directorial shake-up, the dance at the gym forever lost his final imprint.) When Wise and Robbins were called up jointly to the Academy Awards stage—having beaten out the directors Stanley Kramer (*Judgment at Nuremberg*), Robert Rossen (*The Hustler*), Lee Thompson (*The Guns of Navarone*), and Federico Fellini (*La Dolce Vita*)—the two men did not acknowledge each other at all. Wise spoke first, giving a single sentence of anodyne general thanks, and then Jerry, in his extremely soft-spoken, slightly New York–tinged voice, said simply: "I'd like to thank the producers of the movie and also the producers of the original play, Hal Prince and the late Bobby Griffiths. Thank you."

It was actually the second appearance onstage for Robbins, who had earlier been awarded a special Academy Award for choreographic achievement, handed to him by Gene Kelly. Jerome Robbins could not know it then, but this evening was to mark the pinnacle of his movie career. He had sacrificed a great deal to get to Hollywood (it is one of the reasons always given for his capitulation to HUAC), yet he never made another movie after this one. Still, he did manage to have an extraordinary impact on the general culture through this one film alone. For it is as the director and choreographer of *West Side Story* that Jerome Robbins is still famous; it is the one thing about him that everyone now remembers. In fact, even Leonard Bernstein, to his distress, came to be known during his lifetime mainly as the composer of *West Side Story*. It was the kind of overwhelming public success that no one involved could escape from.

And Robbins didn't necessarily want to escape. Lenny may have had more exclusively classical aspirations, but Jerry lacked that kind of brow-level snobbery: he believed that the "popular theater," as he called it, could also be the home of art. By 1959 he had demonstrated this with a third hit, *Gypsy*—not as magical in its execution nor as unusual in its conception as *Peter Pan* and *West Side Story*, but still an enduring favorite with critics and audience members alike. Theater people, in particular, are likely to forgive the plot its longueurs because it is a story about them, about their lives onstage and backstage and the pain it caused them to get there. And Jerry was no stranger to that position, for *Gypsy* in some ways represented a version of *his* life as well. He was neither as ignored nor as manipulated as Louise was as a child, but like Louise, he had willfully wrested his onstage achievements and his new name from the hands of a grudging mother. And like Mama Rose, Jerry's parents had ultimately come around to viewing his victory as their own. If his notable accomplishments and great financial success left him feeling hollow at times, they were nonetheless essential to his sense of self. Broadway had been his salvation, and by the beginning of the 1960s he considered himself at least as committed to his particular form of musical theater as the stripper Gypsy Rose Lee was to hers.

Fiddler on the Roof

WHEN HE WAS nearly six years old, in the summer of 1924, Jerry and his twelve-year-old sister were taken by their mother to visit their paternal grandfather in his native village of Rozhanka. The shtetl had been transferred from Russia to Poland when the borders moved after the First World War, and its name had officially been changed to Rejanke, but otherwise it still very much resembled the place from which Jerry's father, as a seventeen-year-old seeking to avoid conscription in the tsar's army, had emigrated in 1904.

For the little boy from New Jersey, Rozhanka was an idyllic location, with a grandfather who loved him dearly and sang lullabies to him every night, plus plenty of village children to play with, horses to ride instead of automobiles to watch out for, and novel activities like fishing in brooks and climbing in haylofts. That summer was to remain a golden period in his imagination for the rest of his life. "They told me I spoke Yiddish there and that I played with the children of the shtetl all day long in the fields, in the yards. . . . I remember tea, candles, jams and the melodies of voices. It was lovely, all lovely. I do not remember one unhappy moment there," he recalled.

Though the shtetl must have been surrounded by a hostile or at least indifferent Christian community, Jerry's memories of it retained not a whiff of anti-Semitism. Prior to his trip to Poland, and in the teenage years that followed it, his experience of Judaism was to be much more mixed. Some of the problems came from the outside. When he was practicing at home for his bar mitzvah, for instance, a group of neighborhood boys who were not Jewish (and who he had thought were his friends) jeered at him through the window and then came into the house, unimpeded by the rabbi who was there to tutor him. It was Jerry, humiliated and angry, who had to yell at them to leave. So his bar mitzvah itself was, in his own mind, a compromised and embarrassing rather than celebratory occasion.

But part of Jerome Rabinowitz's complicated relation to his own Jewishness, a complication that was to extend throughout his life, stemmed from inside the family. His memories of evening meals in Weehawken were eons away from the lit candles and gentle songs of Rozhanka. "Sonia and Mother. Pots would be slammed, voices rise; I'll make it myself—my way, your way—aggravation—that killer disease caused by children of martyred parents—smell of onions, eggs & lox frying—challah toasted—a constant going & coming to the table for plates, salt, butter—the meal being eaten piecemeal—the fight going on," and on, and on, until finally his father, "like Jove, hurls his Yiddish thunderbolts," and the argument subsides. And though he was told he had spoken Yiddish himself in Poland, here in America there were instead family celebrations with "the yiddish jokes I could not understand," forcing him to join in the adults' laughter without really knowing what he was laughing at. Though he blamed himself later for rejecting a heritage that was "subtly, subtly" offered to him, "more gently than I ever realized," with "the superstitions, the temperaments, the fears and the glorious good times, the celebrations, foods, inflexions, songs," his experience at the time was actually something much darker and less easily lovable.

As an adult, he would encounter other forms of Jewishness that seemed more appealing. In 1951, for example, he made his first trip to Israel on a grant from the American Fund for Israel Institutions, and he was profoundly touched by what he saw there. He visited dance companies and dance festivals, watched plays and operas produced in Jewish theaters, toured archaeological sites and kibbutzim, attended a Yemenite wedding, and even got together with the members of the extended Rabinowitz family who had left Rozhanka for Israel. It was not only seeing the culture "develop right under your eyes" and finding folk dance choreographers who were "still alive and creative" that moved him. He was responding to Israel not just as a dancer-choreographer, but with a part of himself that had up till then been kept in abeyance. As he wrote to Tanaquil Le Clercq, "It felt like home, and made me very proud to be a Jew; something I always negated and rejected."

Years later, in 1959, when he took his Ballets: USA company on a tour that included Tel Aviv, he attended a Sabbath celebration at a Hasidic synagogue, where he found himself so inspired by the ecstatic dancing that he got up and joined right in. "One day I'm going to make a ballet out of that," he told a friend.

In the summer of 1963, Robbins was shown the script of a musical based on the stories of the Yiddish writer Sholem Aleichem. The book was by Joseph Stein, the lyrics were by Sheldon Harnick, and the music was by Jerry Bock—a team whose greatest success to date had been the 1959 Broadway musical *Fiorello!* Their new work followed the shtetl life of the Russian-Jewish milkman Tevye, his wife, Golde, and their three marriageable daughters, Tzeitel, Hodel, and Chava. Perhaps in exclamatory imitation of the trio's earlier theatrical triumph, it bore the title *To Life!*

Despite his ever-growing popularity as a Broadway director, Robbins happened to be free of other obligations at the time. His two recent ventures into straight theater—first Arthur Kopit's *Oh Dad, Poor Dad, Mamma's Hung You in the Closet and I'm Feelin' So Sad*, and then Bertolt Brecht's *Mother Courage*— had both ended their runs, and he had recently given up the directorship of the Fanny Brice/Barbra Streisand musical that was to become *Funny Girl*. But though he was available, he was getting a bit weary of Broadway, and he told Joseph Stein that he wasn't interested in "doing another run-of-the-mill musical." Still, he agreed to sit down for an audition, and after a sampling of the songs and parts of the new script, he became enthusiastic. "I'M GOING TO DO A MUSICAL OF SHOLEM ALEICHEM STORIES WITH HARNICK AND BOCK STOP I'M IN LOVE WITH IT IT'S OUR PEOPLE," he instantly cabled to Ruth Mitchell, his usual stage manager; and then, in a further effort to bring her on board, he followed this up with: "IT'S THE ONLY SHOW SINCE WEST SIDE STORY THAT HAS ME REALLY EXCITED."

"Our people"—that is, Jews—accounted for a vast proportion of the show's backers and creators, and there were the usual mordant jokes, as the production moved forward, about how to present the topic so that it would attract more than a Hadassah audience. That, it seemed, was the inherent danger of the material: the same thing that drew Robbins and his colleagues might be precisely what would blind them to its limitations, for they were in love with the subject itself and with its connection to their own pasts. Of no one was this more true than of Jerry. The project not only reactivated his childhood memories of idyllic Rozhanka; it also offered him a chance to come to grips with his own tortured connection to Jewishness

—including his heretofore somewhat distant relationship with his father. Harry Robbins had remarried and moved to Florida after Lena's 1955 death, so there was now a physical distance as well as an emotional one between him and his son. But Jerry overcame it, spending hours down there interviewing his father about family history and shtetl life. As with all his theatrical projects (including his ballet projects), he clearly wanted this production to be *true* in some way as well as lyrical and appealing.

What all the participants remembered was how Robbins constantly harped at them to get the focus right. "What's the show *about?*" he kept asking, and was never satisfied with their simple plot summaries. His interrogations became so decidedly Talmudic that The Boys (as he called Stein, Harnick, and Bock) began to address him as Reb Robbins. The process may have seemed unduly wearisome, but when they finally gave him the answer he wanted—the erosion of a traditional way of life— and he in turn insisted on an opening number that focused on that theme (which turned out to be the song "Tradition"), they all saw the point of the long inquisition. It was precisely his relentlessness that made him so valuable as their director.

And he carried this same method of constant scrutiny and correction into every aspect of the show. It was said, for instance, that he restaged the Sabbath dinner scene twenty times or more, just to get everyone's placement and action right. He tortured the actors with his critiques of their performances (Austin Pendleton being the most extreme example), and he even dared to give notes to Zero Mostel, who had been chosen to play the lead role. Mostel and Robbins were never going to be friends, given Jerry's HUAC testimony, but they had gotten over the worst of the barrier when Robbins stepped in to script-doctor *A Funny Thing Happened on the Way to the Forum* and Mostel leveled his "loose lips" crack in public. For this new musical, Jerry actively pursued the actor, flattering him with the idea (which may have been true) that he was the only one who could really play Tevye. "Dear Zee, please don't make me do this without you. Please," he wrote imploringly.

Robbins's ambitions for the show were so vast that he even asked the world-famous Jewish artist Marc Chagall to design the sets. Chagall politely declined, but a detail from one of his pictures—the fiddler on the roof—ended up appearing at the beginning and the end of the musical, a small but important addition that also provided the work's final, seemingly predestined name. Instead of Chagall, Robbins hired the gifted Boris Aronson, who translated Jerry's explicit and detailed notes into evocative, hallucinatory sets, meanwhile complaining constantly about Jerry's dictatorial manner. The costumes, too, were subject to Robbins's direct supervision: he wanted Patricia Zipprodt to make them poorer-looking and less glamorous than the ones she originally submitted to him. The look and feel of the Eastern European shtetl was part of what he was seeking, as he pored over research materials like Roman Vishniac's photographs of Polish Jews and films like *The Dybbuk*. Even the dance culture got thoroughly researched, as Robbins, with the help of the Orthodox dance scholar Dvora Lapson, sought out and attended Hasidic weddings in order to observe the men's steps and gestures. And none other than Jerry's original dance "rabbi," his mentor Gluck Sandor, was enlisted to play a rabbi in the show.

The production ran into all the usual problems and then some—not just a runaway producer, Fred Coe, who had to be replaced by Hal Prince in the early fall of 1963, but also the assassination of President Kennedy on November 22, an event so profoundly disturbing that it interrupted auditions for the show, even as it also darkened every theater on Broadway. For those involved in *Fiddler on the Roof*, this national tragedy must have reinforced their sense that the history of loss and the terror of displacement were still pertinent subjects, even in childishly optimistic America. One might argue, in fact, that the Kennedy assassination made fearful Jews out of everyone, or at the very least made the average non-Jewish American more conscious of the catastrophes that life could deal out.

But success with an audience was never guaranteed. The following summer, during the lengthy out-of-town run-up to the Broadway opening, *Fiddler on the Roof* was still struggling to overcome its stodgy tedium. The Detroit critics called the show "lacklustre," "serviceable," and "pedestrian." "Jerry, what are you going to do?" Austin Pendleton asked him, as they got ready to begin their final tryouts, a month-long series of performances in Washington, D.C. "Ten things a day," Jerry answered him, and that's what he did. Dialogue was cut; songs were cut. Most painfully for Robbins, even dances were cut, including an entire dream-ballet that was meant to signal Chava's separation from her family after her marriage to a non-Jew. But dance numbers were also added at this point—crucially, a "bottle dance" for Hasidic men that Robbins had been working on since Detroit, and which he perfected and added to the performances in Washington. Placed at the end of the first act, during Tzeitel's wedding to Motel, it was exactly the kind of showstopper the production had needed all along. "Any man who can do that," said the put-upon Boris Aronson, after seeing the dance performed for the first time, "I forgive everything."

Fiddler on the Roof opened on Broadway on September 22, 1964, and it was obvious from the audience reaction that it was going to be an instant hit. At the party Hal Prince threw afterward at the Rainbow Room, everyone was so confident and joyous that the official reviews were merely icing on the cake. Perhaps the most important review, for Jerry, had already come in from his father, who went backstage after the performance "and threw his arms around me and wept and wept and said how did I know all that."

The only dissenting voice came from the *Herald Tribune*'s

Walter Kerr, who wrote, "I think it might be an altogether charming musical, if only the people of Anatevka did not pause every now and then to give their regards to Broadway, with remembrances to Herald Square." And though Jerry should have been inured to negative reviews by this time, he was cut to the quick by this otherwise positive one. Apparently he even drafted a letter (which he never sent) explaining to Kerr that it was by *eliminating* dance numbers, rather than by adding in excessive glitz, that he had enabled the show to reach Broadway. Perhaps what really upset him about the article was that he sensed, on some level, that Kerr might be right. Even at the pinnacle of his Broadway achievement, he may have realized that popular success, for a musical, was likely to be proportionate to the coarseness of its approach and the heavy-handed emotionalism with which it bludgeoned its audiences. And whether he realized this or not, he acted on it, for *Fiddler* was to be the last new musical he ever directed.

We can, of course, have no direct access to that original production, with Zero Mostel as the lead, hand-picked actors even in the smaller roles, and Robbins's influence evident behind every movement and scene. The 1971 movie, directed by Norman Jewison, preserves some of Jerry's choreography but is otherwise in no way a Robbins project. Jewison's movie, at nearly three hours, now comes across as a prolonged exercise in sentimental cliché (despite Pauline Kael's incomprehensible insistence that it was "the most *powerful* film musical ever made").

But though the film may flatten the theatrical experience, it is not totally untrue to it. *Fiddler on the Roof* simply contains too much boring narrative to be worked through, in proportion to the few redeeming moments of song and the even more redeeming (but even fewer) moments of dance. To call the plot "schematic" is to flatter it. We must sit by as all three of Tevye's daughters are married off in turn, each choosing a suitor less and less to her father's taste, until finally the last one marries a Gentile and is banished from the family forever. Even those of us who stem from the same Russian-Jewish background being depicted on the screen are likely to feel "So enough already!" by the middle of the turgid second act. If *West Side Story* is great in part because it had the shortest book on record—choosing to convey everything through dance and song instead of words— *Fiddler* suffers from the opposite tendency, an excessive reliance on explicit verbiage.

Some of that problem may stem from the creators' understandably respectful attitude toward their source material. Converting Sholem Aleichem's much-loved short stories to a script is not the same as commissioning an Arthur Laurents work-for-hire; one cuts at one's peril. But some of the problem, surely, had to do with those same creators' blinkered affection for the Jewish subject matter. They were *all* doing it for their fathers (or grandfathers, or assorted relatives, living and dead), and as a result they were able to accept declarative statements in place of felt experience, formulaic fairy tales presented as history, and schmaltz instead of real feeling. *Fiddler on the Roof* is the only production by Jerome Robbins that actually exhibits to a disturbing degree the vulgarity and simplemindedness his plot-filled dances were sometimes charged with. When he was dealing with pure dance (or even impure dance, since he loved to mix things up), Jerry was able to counter the vulgarity with something sharper and stronger: something like self-analysis, or profound questioning, or mutually acknowledged awareness. But faced with this ultimately one-dimensional material, his capacity for astute observation deserted him.

The exceptions are the major dance numbers. In two distinct places, the tedious plot gives way to—is, indeed, completely overridden by—the vitality of dramatic movement to music. The first of these is an encounter between Jews and Cossacks at the local drinking spot where Tevye has gone to confer with a well-to-do merchant about a possible marriage to one of his daughters. As the two men are sitting and drinking among their fellow Jews, a group of Cossacks enters the tavern, and the dance that results, with waves of show-offy squat kicks taking over the stage, only to be repelled briefly by a more hesitant Jewish line dance, resembles nothing so much as Robbins's Dance at the Gym from *West Side Story*. Here is cultural opposition presented theatrically, at long last; and here is fear, a rare emotion in dance, made palpable through aggressively choreographed movement.

The second and even better passage is the famous Bottle Dance that closes both the eldest daughter's wedding celebration and the show's first act. It begins when four black-hatted men, identically garbed in long black coats and full beards, place wine bottles on top of their hats and proceed to do a delicate but also emphatic dance to klezmer music. At first they are merely gesturing individually with their hands and arms (standard Jewish gestures of a "Praise God!" and "Who, me?" sort), but soon they are arrayed in a line where they rise up on tiptoe, or tap their heels and toes, or crawl forward on their knees and then triumphantly stand up again, all in unison. Though the dance looks entirely Jewish, many of the steps are taken directly from ballet (as in the "piqués" that the men do when they move sideways on their toes); yet the movement has been so thoroughly disguised, by both the music and the theatrical direction, that it doesn't look balletic at all. This four-man bottle dance then segues into an even wilder dance involving eight additional identically black-clad men who twirl and swirl around the dance-space with the original four, until finally all twelve are bound together in a whirling circle, hands clasped behind each other's backs as they revolve to the emphatically rhythmic clapping of all the onlookers, male and female. The whole segment is a piercing joy to watch, and it ends the first act with a bang.

Perhaps because he had been forced to cut other, similarly powerful dances from the musical, Robbins found himself unable to let go of Jewish dance, even after he finished with *Fiddler* and retreated fulltime to the world of ballet. He did not pursue his further exploration right away. First he let nearly a decade go by, during which he choreographed what may well be his most classical, his least "ethnic" dances for the New York City Ballet. But in 1973 he returned to an idea he had broached as early as 1951: *The Dybbuk*, the plot which Balanchine had rejected and Lincoln Kirstein had suggested he take to the Batsheva Dance Company instead. Once again he turned to his original collaborator on this venture, Leonard Bernstein, and together they turned out a work that premiered in 1974.

The Dybbuk—or *Dybbuk Variations*, which is the later, tinkered-with form in which the dance survived—does not really represent Robbins at his best. Derived from a 1914 play by the Russian-Jewish writer S. Ansky, the plot involves a young Hasidic couple who are scheduled to marry, until the young man dies; then he invades the body of his beloved as a "dybbuk," or demon, preventing her from marrying another and eventually causing her death. None of this complex plot is readily apparent in the dance that came out of it. While one can detect a certain amount of Jewish-style gesture at the beginning and the end, along with a discernible merging of male with female, black-costumed figures with white, as the central couple moves toward its deadly apotheosis, the narrative is never made as graspable as it is in, say, *The Cage*. That earlier ballet did not need to be fully understood on a plot level to succeed (one might argue that it *couldn't* be fully understood, if it was to succeed fully), and clearly Robbins was hoping for a similar degree of latitude here. But whereas his best ballets are simultaneously ambiguous and clear, *Dybbuk Variations* just feels muddy and somehow inscrutable, as if it were purposely withholding its own story from us.

The dance has more wrong with it than simple confusion. *Dybbuk* includes lots of gesture and pose-holding, but surprisingly little actual dance; and when the moments of real dance do emerge, their mesh with the Bernstein music feels incomplete and unsatisfactory. Unlike Bernstein's previous compositions for Robbins, the piece itself, though it perhaps works in concert form, seems largely unsuited to dance. Perhaps this was because Jerry and Lenny worked mainly apart on this, not together as they had done in *West Side Story* and *Fancy Free*. But perhaps it was also a matter of their complicated relationship to their own Jewishness. For each of them, though in different ways, this project felt somehow obligatory: a belated payment due to the partially rejected heritage, a gesture of familial or tribal appeasement.

Such motives are not conducive to the production of good art, and one would have to list *The Dybbuk* among Robbins's brave failures. But even with its shortcomings, it has moments of interest and power, particularly in the brief demonic solos of some of the men. And it did not deserve the vituperative response of Arlene Croce—always Robbins's harshest critic— who wrote scathingly about the absence of the original play's "explosive, archaic passions" and asked: "Is this what he's been waiting thirty years to do—to cut the guts out of a great old Russian-Yiddish primitive beast?"

While he was reworking *The Dybbuk* into *Dybbuk Variations*, attempting to make it into less of an incompletely staged drama and more of a pure dance sequence, Robbins came across a book called *The Ordeal of Civility*, written by a man named John Murray Cuddihy and published by Basic Books in 1974. It is a curious book for Jerry to have read—densely written, sometimes verging on the incomprehensible, and seriously academic in its approach—but his marginal notes suggest that he read it thoroughly, particularly the section about Freud. Subtitled *Freud, Marx, Lévi-Straus, and the Jewish Struggle with Modernity,* the book purports to examine the question of how Jewish intellectuals blended into modern European culture by, essentially, erasing their Jewishness.

The text has many byways and digressions—the twenty-one epigraphs alone, ranging from Thomas Hobbes, Talcott Parsons, and Max Weber to Erving Goffman, Norman Mailer, and Hannah Arendt, could take a lifetime to unwrap—but its essential message is that "civility" was a disguise Jews took on to make themselves palatable to a wider Protestant culture. A few sentences chosen nearly at random (similar ones occur throughout the book) will serve to illustrate Cuddihy's point. "What was normal in the shtetl *Gemeinschaft,*" Cuddihy writes, "looked bad in the West. Jewry, in general, was making a 'scene' in *Gesellschaft,* and everybody knew it, though few would admit it: the Jews were too ashamed, the liberal Gentiles too 'nice.'" Or: "The rights and duties of the *citoyen* integrated the Jew into a remote solidarity with the Gentile West. . . . The social skills for negotiating such solidarity must be learned, often, by mingling with members of bourgeois society itself. This was especially difficult for a 'pariah people' closed out from social solidarity with respectable society because it was deemed wanting in respectability in the first place." Chapters bear titles like "'Passing' into the West," "The Guilt of Shame," "The Ancient *Judenfrage,*" and "Sexuality and Christianity: The Refining Process." The embarrassment of a vulgar Jewish sexuality is brought to the fore: great weight, for instance, is placed on the fact that "Freud was at once proud and deeply troubled by the fact that it was he, a Jew, who had discovered the sexual etiology of the neuroses."

One can see how this kind of thing might have grabbed Jerry's attention, addressing, as it seemed to do, his own tortured relationship to the larger American culture, in which he had so often found his successes to be hollow and unpersuasive. Among the many ironies—though, again, it was typical of Robbins's built-in inferiority complex—was the fact that it was a *non*-Jew's book about Jews that attracted him. Though *The Ordeal of Civility* had been respectfully reviewed in the mainstream media, it had also become a kind of battle-flag for white supremacist readers, who felt that Cuddihy, a lapsed Catholic, was finally outing the Jews who had been "passing" as civilized people. "Cuddihy is to be credited for one of history's more thoroughgoing, if obscure, exposures of Jewish deception," wrote a New York attorney named Hugh Lincoln, in a review titled "Id of the Yid: Our Apoplectic Invaders Considered" that appeared in a magazine called *National Vanguard* around the time Robbins was discovering the book. Imagine, if you will, a text by a white man that purported to explain how the incivility, bad public behavior, and overt sexuality of black people could only be countered by the minority race's concerted decision to blend in with the dominant culture's manners. That, in essence, was the line Cuddihy was taking, though he spoke mainly in terms borrowed from the enlightenment Jews themselves, who had always been the first to critique their own personalities and their own tribal mores.

It was this bizarre if scholarly-seeming document which caused Robbins to sink ever deeper into realms of self-torture and self-doubt. After reading Cuddihy, Jerry began to question his whole relationship to dance—almost, it seems, his whole relationship to his body. At times he explicitly associated this forced civility ("civilizationing," he called it) with the practice of ballet. "I affect a discipline over my body," he wrote in a journal in 1976, "and take on another language . . . the language of court and christianity—church & state—a completely artificial convention of movement—one that deforms and reforms the body & imposes a set of artificial conventions of beauty—a language *not* universal." And he went on to ask himself "what wondrous & monstrous" kinds of movement would emerge "if I would dig down to my Jew self."

But in taking this line, Robbins was willfully turning against everything that had actually made him the choreographer he was. It was precisely his sense of exclusion—his awareness that every dance form, including ballet, had its own conventions that could be chronicled and analyzed and made new by looking at it from the outside—which had enabled him to make dances ranging from the March of the Siamese Children to *Afternoon of a Faun* to the Dance at the Gym to the Bottle Dance in *Fiddler*. He was no more a "Jew self," in dance terms, than he was a ballet self or a Puerto Rican self or a Siamese self. Each of these different dance forms had attracted him with its novelty, its exoticism, its otherness in comparison to routine daily gesture; and it was the difficult but successful effort to integrate each kind of dance with non-dance movement that most distinguished him as a choreographer. He could only do the work he did, of blending varying kinds of dance across cultures, across brow levels, and across stage venues, because he was, first and foremost, an outsider. And it was because he at least partially viewed himself as an insider to Jewishness, as someone who ought to speak its language naturally, that he remained largely unable to express that culture effectively through dance. Only the hybrid, mixed-together forms, it turned out—the Hasidic dance built on piqués, the ballet that drew on natural human movement—ultimately served him well.

Dances at a Gathering

For the greater part of a decade, Robbins had been making Broadway hits, ranging from *Peter Pan* and *West Side Story* through *Gypsy* and *Fiddler on the Roof*. He had also been running his own dance troupe, Ballets: USA, which successfully toured throughout Europe, and for whom he choreographed both popular dances like *NY Export: Opus Jazz* and serious, somewhat difficult dances like *Moves*. Meanwhile, he had begun directing the American premieres of non-musical plays—Brecht's *Mother Courage*, Kopit's *Oh Dad, Poor Dad*— even as he was script-doctoring and improving the musical comedies put on by others. He had also, in his usual fashion, been carrying on a wild social life that ranged between women (the actress Zohra Lampert was one) and men (a series of actors and dancers, most of whom were significantly younger than Jerry). He had not, in other words, settled down to either a single profession or a single partner.

Nor was he about to. When *Fiddler*'s assured success left him free to turn to other projects, he first took up Lucia Chase's invitation to choreograph something for his old company, American Ballet Theatre. His choice was Stravinsky's *Les Noces*, a massive production which had first been done in 1923 by Bronislava Nijinska, Nijinsky's sister. (Nijinska had, perhaps not incidentally, been a ballet teacher of Jerry's during his early years at ABT, although, as he later confided to an interviewer, "she took a sort of instant dislike to me when I walked in on the first day . . . it was very hard for me to work with her.") Robbins's *Les Noces*, when it premiered in 1965, was notably unlike Nijinska's, which he professed not to have seen at that point, though it did share with its predecessor a faithful attention to Stravinsky's score and a strong sense of the ritual entailed in a village wedding. The performance marked, at any rate, his triumphant return to the world of ballet after a complete four-year absence, garnering a strong positive response in New York as well as an expressed interest in remounting it on the part of several foreign ballet companies. Robbins himself apparently did not consider it one of his complete successes: "It's a little athletic," he wrote to the English poet Robert Graves, "more so than I wanted it to be, and I think that this is because of my overzealous attempt to communicate *everything* about what I heard and saw in the music."

Soon after this, he began working on two theatrical projects simultaneously: the staging of a new play by María Irene Fornés called *The Office*, and a collaboration with Bernstein on a long-planned musical production of Thornton Wilder's play *The Skin of Our Teeth*. Both of these efforts had come quite far along before they faltered; neither, for one reason or another, ever made it to the stage. But by 1966 Robbins had another drama-related venture to occupy his interest. Less than a year after the September 1965 formation of the new National Endowment for the Arts, Jerome Robbins received one of the first large grants (it was for $300,000, a tenth of the NEA's initial budget) to set up something he called the American Theatre Laboratory. Aimed at a handful of auditioned theater professionals—eleven participants to begin with, and fluctuating numbers thereafter—it entailed two years of full-day, five-day-a-week exercises and explorations in various versions of theater craft. The aim was not to come up with a finished production, but to generate ideas about theater. In pursuit of this admirable goal, Robbins brought in (among many other things) Noh drama practices, Gravesian ideas from *The White Goddess*, ancient Greek choruses, Japanese tea ceremonies, Polish "poor theater," movement classes taught by Anna Sokolow, music sessions with Leonard Bernstein, and designs by the young Robert Wilson, who was just starting up his own downtown productions. The participants in ATL were asked to do various strange things, from taking on the characters of different animals to participating in paint-ball fights, which were supposed to free up the creative juices. It was all very 1960s, very much of its time, though perhaps in a more intense and directed way than the usual "happenings" of this period; and just about everyone who was part of the project remembered the two-year experiment with enormous affection.

This late-1960s interlude, which carried far less pressure than the Broadway life, gave Robbins a chance to relax socially and enjoy his connections with friends and lovers. He had been renting a summer place in the elegant and exclusive community of Snedens Landing, a few miles up the Hudson from New York, and there he met a family—the psychoanalyst Daniel Stern, his wife, Ann, and the Sterns' two children—who became a kind of surrogate family for Jerry. He also socialized with Bob Wilson and his partner, and with Grover Dale, a young performer from *West Side Story* who had become his trusted assistant at ATL. His long-term friendship with Tanny Le Clercq intensified when her troubles with Balanchine, who was publicly obsessed with Suzanne Farrell, caused her to begin writing to Jerry in a more passionate vein; and in October of 1967 she threw him a glorious forty-ninth birthday dinner. But just as Tanny seemed possibly about to become more available, Robbins turned his attentions to a new flame, Christine Conrad, with whom he began an affair in 1967 (though not without diverging from it, as he always did, to pursue a male lover—in this case a handsome, elusive man named Richard).

He also, in 1967, bought the townhouse at 117 East Eighty-First Street where he was to spend the rest of his life. By this time Robbins was quite well-to-do, and he had freely spent part of his show-biz wealth on a Florida condominium for his father and stepmother. But it was unlike him to spend large amounts of money on himself, and he would probably have been satisfied to remain in his Seventy-Fourth Street rental, where he had long occupied an apartment within a house owned by Muriel Resnick. Resnick, however, having recently made her own small fortune on a successful play, had apologetically taken back the whole house for herself, so Jerry was forced to move. The Eighty-First Street house was big enough so that it could accommodate, among other things, an office occupied by his longtime secretary Edith Weissman, who had managed his business affairs since the early 1950s. (Over the years, Edith was to prove one of his dearest and most loyal associates, and as a token of his gratitude and affection he would eventually, in 1978, grant her the royalties from *Afternoon of a Faun*.) Weissman handled all his routine correspondence, scheduling, and day-to-day concerns; more technical tasks, including contracts, permissions, investments, and bequests, were outsourced to his lawyer, Flora Lasky, and his financial advisor, Allen Greenberg.

The house also offered ample room for his beloved dogs, who—one at a time, or occasionally in pairs—occupied a central place in his life. Jerry's letters and journals often included references to these pets, and he was known to view them as an extension of his intimate social circle. Nick, for instance (a somewhat later addition to his household), was a wirehaired terrier mix given to him as a birthday present by his close friend Slim Keith; the dog's name often came up in Jerry's notes to and about human friends, as if he were simply one of their number. Some of the other dogs who appeared in his life over the decades were named Snuff, Annie, and Tess.

In addition to making life more luxurious for its succession of canine inhabitants, the townhouse allowed Robbins plenty of room for entertaining friends, colleagues, and lovers. He even gave Chris Conrad her own space in the building, which she was to occupy for the two years of their relationship, only moving out when the parallel affair with Richard became impossible for her to ignore.

Among its other advantages, the Eighty-First Street townhouse had a top floor that was perfect for a ballet studio. Little did Robbins know, when he acquired it, how useful such a rehearsal and choreographic space would become, for when he first moved into the house he was still deeply immersed in his ATL work. It would take a couple more years before his life caught up with his house, and ballet returned to the center of it.

In early 1969 Lincoln Kirstein issued one of his regular invitations to Jerry to return to the New York City Ballet and choreograph new work for the dancers. This time, though, the invitation had an urgency it had not previously possessed. The company was facing its twenty-fifth anniversary gala on May 8, and it desperately needed good new work. Meanwhile, the master choreographer had gone, if not AWOL, then at least slightly astray in his unhappy pursuit of Suzanne Farrell, which seriously interfered with both his productivity and his relations with the rest of the company. With Balanchine in semi-abeyance, then, Robbins became more necessary than ever, and he rose to the challenge.

He began by working with just one couple, Edward Villela and Patricia McBride, whom he had earlier coached in *Afternoon of a Faun* in the top-floor ballet studio of his house. Now, however, *he* was coming to *them*—and at an unfamiliar location, the New York State Theater at Lincoln Center, to which NYCB had moved in 1966 from its old City Center location. Nervous about how he would fit in with the new members of the company after such a long time away, Robbins at first chose to work with dancers he already knew. However, he soon expanded his group to six dancers, and eventually to ten. These included five women (Allegra Kent, Sara Leland, Kay Mazzo, Patricia McBride, and Violette Verdy) and five men (Anthony Blum, John Clifford, Robert Maiorano, John Prinz, and Edward Villela). Each of them was to play a specific role, but a role defined entirely by costume color—the Girl in Apricot (or Green, or Mauve), the Boy in Brown (or Mustard, or Plum). Due to the complicated rehearsal schedule at NYCB, he couldn't always assemble all the dancers when he wanted them, so the dance he was working on was composed in bits and pieces, with most segments involving only a fraction of the total ten. He seemed, in fact, to be working slowly toward something without knowing exactly what it would be.

"In an empty studio, when you start a ballet, and the first dancer begins, it's rather an awesome moment, because it's like putting the first mark of ink on a piece of blank paper," Robbins told his friend Rosamond Bernier in a 1986 interview. "Where it starts: because from then on your whole pattern is going to be connected to that—your whole structure, I should say. And I always feel choreography is a little like building a bridge such as could not happen anywhere else, which is that you start on one side and you build a step, and then you build another step and another step, and the bridge is sort of arced out over nothing. And the structure of it has to contain itself, so it meets at the end of the ballet, and it makes an architectural structure which is satisfying."

Usually, when he choreographed, Robbins had the underlying structure of the musical score to guide him. But in this case he was working with separate piano pieces by Chopin, and it was not at all clear in what order they should go. All he knew, to begin with, was that it must be Chopin solo piano, because that was the music he had heard long ago in his ballet classes, the standard accompaniment to his and all other ballet dancers' training. That this music was a strange mixture in itself—a solo voice standing in for a whole orchestra, at once Polish and French, retaining its roots in traditional folk tunes while also defining a form of romantic classicism—would have stimulated his own choreographic tendency to mix modes. And perhaps the work he had recently done on *Fiddler* helped him to hear those folk roots more clearly, even as his long absence from the world of ballet drew him to the classical style he had missed.

In Robbins's choreographic history there was one obvious predecessor to this new Chopin dance, and that was the 1956 piece he titled *The Concert; or, The Perils of Everybody*. Set to a series of unlisted Chopin piano works backed by a full orchestra, *The Concert* is an overtly comic ballet. The mugging begins right at the start, when the pianist strides onto the stage to orchestral accompaniment, bows to the audience as the orchestra falls silent, grandiosely seats himself at the piano, theatrically dusts off his keyboard with a handkerchief, and then glares at the snickering audience. As he starts to play his first Chopin tune, a series of dancers emerge from the wings in solos and pairs and seat themselves in the folding chairs they have carried on. All are basically outfitted in blue leotards and tights—in other words, as ballet dancers—but each also wears a few accoutrements that define his or her character: a beret and scarf for the self-styled artist, fancy hats for some of the society women, white collars, ties, and even jackets for some of the men, a knit cap for a bag-lady type, horn-rimmed glasses for an intellectual, and long, flowing hair for a particularly music-besotted female who drapes herself over the piano and later performs in a frenzied duet. (In its original incarnation, this role was played by Tanaquil Le Clercq.) When the actual dancing starts, it is mock-dancing, with extremes of awkwardness and noticeable failures to keep in step. At one point the men pick up the women and carry them around as if they were furniture, or store mannequins, or perhaps folding chairs. Umbrellas get opened and closed under imaginary rain. A "butterfly" man in wings and antennae (though still wearing the horn-rimmed glasses he sported earlier) dances with a woman in a similar outfit; they are joined by a swarm of the same kind, all flapping their arms. At one point a fallen body gets left in the middle of the stage; it soon gets removed. Finally the pianist bangs his piano keys in frustration, gets up from the piano, and moves toward the dancers with a butterfly net, as if to capture them. Then the foredrop (a painted canvas representing the interior of an auditorium) comes down, and the audience explodes in laughter and applause as the ten stars, the additional ten backup dancers, and the pianist all come out for their curtain calls.

The Concert has been a great success over the years, but it is hardly Robbins at its finest. If you go in for ballet mockery, you can see it done better at a performance of the all-male Ballet Trockadero de Monte Carlo, where serious passion combines with unavoidable satire to create a weird mixture. Here, in contrast, the satire feels forced: these are all terrific dancers faking being bad, and the result is that one feels talked down to. Where *The Cage* questions *and* uses the central principles of ballet to achieve its frightening effects, this dance skewers only easy targets, including pseudo-intellectual art lovers, narcissistic performers, and the essential silliness of ballet style itself.

It seems to assure the audience: *Yes, we too find all this hopping about on toe and lifting up of women and dancing in unison ridiculous, and it's okay if you do too.* Even for an audience member who mistrusts ballet—perhaps especially for such a person—*The Concert* fails to persuade, especially if one watches it more than once.

But that has not prevented it from being an audience favorite, even among the most discerning viewers. The choreographer Mark Morris, who first saw it in a 1980s revival, recalls "the fabulous *The Concert*, which is only funny if you see it every ten years and you forgot about it. You can't see it twice in a row or you'll kill yourself: it's not funny, it's awful. And it's a miracle composition—it's great. You know, that's sort of Edward Gorey-ish, that one."

Still, Robbins himself seemed belatedly to feel the shortcomings of the work, maybe even sensing that he needed to make up for its cavalier tone. So when he set out in 1969 to address Chopin again, he decided to forego the light-comedy mode, instead producing something that, in its serious yet witty tribute to the art of ballet, could pleasurably be watched repeatedly. "More, more—make it like popcorn!" said Balanchine enthusiastically, when Jerry showed him the first twenty-five minutes of what was to become an hour-long dance; and Balanchine, who loved food, demonstrated what he meant by tossing imaginary nuggets toward his mouth: "Keep eating, keep eating!"

Dances at a Gathering, as it turned out, was not just about ballet itself, not just about the way a choreographer could conjure a dance out of thin air. It was also about the specific dancers who made up that initial cast. Dance is, by its very nature, ephemeral, and one can never again see Edward Villela start the whole performance with his marvelous Boy in Brown solo, or kneel to touch the stage in a closing moment of quiet reflectiveness. One can never again watch Violette Verdy perform her remarkable character dance, in which she seems to epitomize wit, idiosyncrasy, and drama (and in which her green costume is perhaps a pun on her last name, so much so that the role of the Girl in Green was forever after alluded to as "the Violette Verdy role"). The live experience of being in the room with these people as they build this bridge-to-nowhere, this architectural wonder, is lost to us forever.

But there are good tapes of that initial cast, as well as of a 1984 revival supervised by Robbins himself and featuring different New York City Ballet dancers, including Kyra Nichols, Maria Calegari, and Joseph Duell, among others; and in these recordings you can see what is great about the ballet. It is by no means dancer-proof, and if the situation is not as bad as Mark Morris thinks it is (*"Dances at a Gathering* was for those people," he asserts, "and I don't think it works very well on anyone else"), it is nonetheless the case that in many of the recent performances done worldwide, the dance has gone slack. The drama, the poignance, does not reside in the steps alone; it has to be instilled in the dancers, ideally by Robbins himself. "He was drawn to dancers who were good actors—in City Ballet as much for *Dances at a Gathering* as for something like *West Side Story Suite*," recalls Emily Coates, who as a young ballet dancer worked with Robbins during the last six years of his life. "You know, when the orange boy is circling the girl in yellow, and it's very playful, it's like there's a theatrical impulse there that is still abstracted—motivation not in terms of character specificity, but motivation in terms of: *There's an interaction going on here*." And in Robbins's instructions, as she recalled, "there was a lot of 'Look at her, damn it! Where are you looking?'"

One is used to thinking of interaction as something that takes place between two people, and certainly that kind of intensity is there in the duets of *Dances at a Gathering*. But one of the fascinating things about this dance is the fluidity with which different numbers of people occupy the stage. It goes from solos to couple dances, from trios to groups of five or six, alternating evenness with oddness in somewhat the manner of *Fancy Free*, though on a much larger and more complicated scale. And, as in *Fancy Free*, there is often a man or a woman left out of the pairings-up. This is not the grand-ballet version of couplehood, with a single pair foregrounded against a corps; it is, instead, an ever-changing contemplation of how multiple bodies might occupy a stage.

A certain amount of dramatic tension is inherent in such arrangements, as Robbins suggested when he described his choreography as focusing not just on the way dancers move, "but the way they move in space—because that's what ballets are about: that volume of space which is the stage. And the drama is how they move in it and around it, or separate from each other, or more come in, or are more on one side of the stage, move forward or backward . . ." For Jerry, that abstracted version of onstage drama may also have corresponded to a more personal sense of human interaction, for in his own experience couples gave way to trios and then, perhaps, to solitude, while larger groups of friends formed and re-formed around him. He seemed to be saying as much in a 1976 notebook entry, where he mused on the circumstances surrounding his 1969 ballet: "Did DaaG come out of a time with Chris? Possibly. Also Richard, Grover, Bob W., the Sterns et al."

The dance itself begins with an empty stage. A single man, in brown pants and a pale, slit-necked, Russian-style shirt, strolls on in silence and continues strolling as the solo piano music begins. The pianist, unlike the show-offy one in *The Concert*, is located offstage somewhere: he is not what we are meant to be watching here. Soon this first man—Edward Villela, in the original cast—starts to dance, as if he is trying out his body in relation to the music and the space. With his increasingly vigorous moves, his dance becomes a solo about the sheer pleasure of dancing, appropriately set to a joyous Chopin mazurka. (This was actually the same mazurka Robbins had given to Le Clercq for her solo in *The Concert*, but he cut that solo from the dance after Tanny got sick and could no longer dance the role; he had, as it were, let it lie fallow all these years, waiting for another fine dancer to give it to.)

After the solo ends and the stage briefly darkens before the next piece, allowing the audience to applaud in its traditional ballet-audience manner, the next two movements focus sequentially on two different male-female couples. But by the time we reach the long fourth movement—which begins with a single woman dancing alone, and then morphs into a brief male solo, then another male solo, then a trio with one man and two women, then a dance for those two women and three other men—we have left behind any sense of firm numbers or distinct arrangements. The way the dancers are introduced in waves and disappear in ripples makes it impossible to keep track of how many of them there are, so that *Dances at a Gathering* seems to contain both more and fewer than its actual ten dancers.

Each individual segment of the dance has its own special delights. In one sequence, for instance, two men enter the stage from opposite sides and proceed to dance their own lively duet, skipping backwards around one another in a circle and then taking various Russian-style poses (or perhaps, given the Chopin, Polish-style poses): hands held to the backs of their heads, heels clicked vigorously in the air. At one point they even perform a quick lift, with one man raising the other in the air. It all has the feel of boys playing, men competing against each other in a suitably masculine way, and yet there is also an undertow of the homoerotic, as if to say: *yes, this too, all this is possible in ballet, and can be taken any way you like.*

Their departure from the stage is followed immediately

by the Violette Verdy solo, a dance clearly made for a strong personality who can convey that character through movement. She prances and extends her leg and turns and points her toe, all the while moving her arms and upper body in a way that frames her clever face, suggesting that this is where the true wit and drama reside. Her movements to Chopin's fast tempo are slow and deliberate, as if she can well afford to let the music flow by underneath her. It is a dance that triumphs over mere dance technique, with the wisdom and experience of the female dancer enabling her to make every tiny gesture seem significant. There is something almost masculine in the way this woman dominates the stage, yet she is distinctly womanly: like all the other women in this dance, she wears a nearly transparent dress over a pale leotard and tights, and the floaty skirt flatters and enhances her every movement.

In *Dances at a Gathering*'s final sequence (which clearly announces itself as an ending, even to those who have never seen it before), the performers come in one at a time, walking, not dancing, as the pianist plays a stately, delicate Chopin nocturne. When there are nine of them onstage, the Boy in Brown—the figure who started the whole dance, an hour earlier, with his solo mazurka—kneels and touches the stage. He keeps his hand there awhile, as the other four men and four women stand watching him. It is as if he is saying: *Here. Here is where it all began, and ends, and starts over again every time.* It is a gesture that brings together the real stage, which is a physical object in the world, and the fabled world of "onstage," which exists only for as long as the performance is taking place. (As such, it might be seen as the dance equivalent to a passage in *Paradise Lost*, where Milton describes the golden apples of Eden as "Hesperian fables true, / If true, here only . . ."— allowing the single word "here" to cover both the fantastic place that is Eden, eternally beyond our reach, and the actual line in the poem, right there before our very eyes.) For Robbins, there was always a special meaning that inhered in the stage itself: the place where everything came to life, the place that gave rise to the full measure of theatrical magic. "Jerry always took us to a theater to rehearse. He always tried to have a stage, even if it was a dinky thing down on Forty-Second Street," recalled one of the dancers who worked with him on *The King and I.* Rehearsal rooms might be all very well for some purposes, but it was the stage that made the imagined real.

During that brief moment when we (and the other dancers) are still focused on the kneeling man, a final woman emerges from the back of the stage, and so nine dancers are turned almost invisibly into ten. Then the Boy in Brown rises from the ground and all ten stand together, looking around at this place where they now find themselves. Their eyes move up, left, right, down, all in unison, as their bodies remain still. At first they move only their gazes, their heads; then they collectively extend their right arms across their bodies; then they move both arms. And now, still in unison, they turn their backs on us and all walk upstage, while the poignantly measured music continues to take its course. The ten figures divide into seemingly casual, random groups—not placed in lines, not paired in couples, just standing in some kind of vague relation to each other. Perhaps they are, at this moment, just people at a gathering. And then they become dancers: the men bow to the women, the women curtsy to the men, they all join together briefly in a circle, and then they separate out into couples, slowly walking arm-in-arm as the music ends.

It was not an ending Robbins came to easily; he didn't know, until he had worked out much of the rest of the dance, that this was how it would close. But as an ending it feels right, and natural, and even inevitable. It turns out to be the exact point at which his choreographic bridge was always destined to come down, the very place the arc-over-nothing was aiming at all along.

When it premiered at the New York State Theater at the gala benefit on May 8, 1969, *Dances at a Gathering* was an instant hit, not only with the audience, but with Balanchine himself, who came backstage, according to Jerry, "and gave me Russian kisses and looked me in the eye and no other comment." And after the press attended the first official performance two weeks later, the reviews were extraordinary. Deborah Jowitt, in the *Village Voice*, described it as "so transparent that through this one dance's complex simplicity you seem to understand what Dance is about." And even the ever-critical Arlene Croce, reviewing *Dances at a Gathering* a year later during its first revival, alluded to it as "the great hit of last season" and "history still in the making." Though she couldn't resist launching her usual dig at Robbins as simply a jumped-up Broadway type (this new dance, she thought, displayed "a rather bogus 'stature,' as if Robbins felt he could no longer impress audiences by being his sunny, funny old self"), she had to concede that "there's no question now that this former whiz kid has the authority to go for the big things in life, or that *Dances* is as amazing a demonstration of his ingenuity in the sixties as *Fancy Free* was in the forties and *Afternoon of a Faun* in the fifties."

Robbins went on to other projects immediately—restagings of *Les Noces* for the Royal Swedish Ballet and *Moves* for the Batsheva Dance Company, the development of *The Dybbuk* for the New York City Ballet, not to mention a prolonged period of work on *The Goldberg Variations*, his masterpiece set to Bach—but meanwhile he continued to focus on Chopin's solo piano music. As early as January of 1970, less than a year after the premiere of *Dances at a Gathering*, he brought forth *In the Night*, a cool, elegant, four-movement piece for three couples.

Set to four Chopin nocturnes (Opus 27, No. 1; Opus 55, Nos. 1 and 2; and Opus 9, No. 2), *In the Night* pays tribute to its music in a far more traditional ballet style than *Dances* does. Two of the three couple dances are almost boringly balletic, as if Robbins is trying to channel Balanchine and failing. When he bursts out into his own style—in the Russian-style gestures of the second movement, for instance, or the combinations of waltzing pairs in the fourth—the dance is better but still not great. It feels very much as if the choreographer is willfully trying to recover a source of inspiration that he has already drunk to its dregs.

Even worse, in some ways, is the twenty-minute *Other Dances* that he choreographed in 1976 for Mikhail Baryshnikov and Natalia Makarova, the newly arrived reigning stars of the New York ballet world. To watch these two amazing dancers perform its series of virtuosic solos, bracketed by gallant, twirling duets at the beginning and end, would have been a great pleasure, of course. But these particular dancers could have created pleasure by performing the phone book, and in a way Robbins was relying too heavily on that. Danced in later years by mere mortals (even terrific mortals like Kyra Nichols and Damian Woetzel), the piece comes across as an inconsequential afterthought about Chopin's waltzes and mazurkas, a pendant to the far more weighty and moving *Dances at a Gathering.* Chopin had served Robbins as well as he possibly could in that 1969 venture, allowing the choreographer to return to New York City Ballet after his long absence with a full measure of triumph. But Chopin's magic, however much it captured his imagination then, seems to have been all used up in that one go. Now Robbins needed to turn to a different composer—a wider, deeper, more all-encompassing composer, one he had cared about for practically his whole life—to produce another piano ballet that would equal and even surpass his *Dances.*

The Goldberg Variations

It starts with the curtain lowered. Offstage to the left, a single spotlit musician sits at a piano and begins to play the first of the thirty-two sections that make up Bach's timeless master-piece, the quiet, delicate "Aria" that functions as the theme from which all the subsequent variations derive. Midway through this initial theme, the curtain rises on two dancers, male and female, who are fancifully garbed in eighteenth-century-style costumes. In slow, stately steps, they move downstage toward us, at first exactly mirroring each other's gestures but then add-ing in small modifications and rhythmic variations of their own. The tiny differences are a warning: what we are looking at will change before we even have time to register what we have seen, and seeming repetitions will never be exact copies of what came before.

The dance that comes forth over the next hour and twenty minutes is far too complicated to grasp fully. You would have to see it a hundred times to notice everything, and still parts of it would escape you, because even as you are focusing on one surprising detail, another and different one is unfolding elsewhere. But though it begs for close attentiveness, *The Goldberg Variations* is never a chore to watch. New felicities arise at every moment; Robbins's inventiveness feels unmatched, except by Bach's. It is one of those rare cases when a choreographer's genius does full justice to the great piece of music on which it builds. Nothing Robbins ever did, not even the wonderful *West Side Story*, can touch the intensity and delirious excitement of this piece.

If you own a recording of the music, you may wonder how the dance can last nearly eighty minutes when even Glenn Gould's glacial pace results in a performance time of about half that. Suffice it to say that Robbins takes every possible repeat— and in the hands of a good pianist, that length nonetheless managed to convey a feeling of sprightliness. The musician needs to pause just enough between sections to indicate the transitions, but not long enough to accommodate applause, which has the lovely side-effect of instilling silence, for the most part, in the otherwise overly demonstrative ballet audience.

The seamlessness of the performance is helped along by the way Robbins deploys his successive waves of dancers. For instance, before the Baroque couple have even finished their theme, a trio of dancers in modern dress wander onto the stage to watch. As the first variation sounds on the piano and the initial couple drift off, the modern trio in turn begin to dance. Such transitions are key to this piece: unlike the downtimes that punctuate many traditional ballets (including Robbins's own *Dances at a Gathering*), the transitions here are part of the dance. Sometimes a single dancer continues from one segment into the next; occasionally three or even four stay on, thus blurring the distinction between movements at the same time as they emphasize differences in mood. As the dance progresses and the variations get more complicated, you can't even say for sure how many dancers occupy each of the separate parts, because a group of six might suddenly be doubled by another six, or a soloist be joined by a trio, or a set of four augmented to ten and then diminished to four again, all while the music sweeps onward.

Pleasing symmetries vie with equally pleasing asymmetries, as when a solo woman dances before six men, or three male dancers successively partner four females. At one point fifteen dancers separate into five intertwining trios, then break apart into gendered groups of seven and eight. Yet these constantly shifting numerical patterns never feel rote or imposed, because the dominant force behind every step, every arm gesture, every inclusion of a new dancer is the music itself. It is all perfectly in keeping and at the same time continually surprising. The steps and gestures derive from ballet but not solely from ballet: there are also discernible elements of courtly dance, Russian folk dance, mime, jazz, and all sorts of other things. The profusion is never excessive; the bravura dancing is never just showing off. It is all *necessary*, though in a way that feels like a free and unforced gift.

There is no distinct break at any point in the dance, but just past the middle things begin to alter. Somewhere around variation sixteen or seventeen, a new form of costuming enters in, and the men—who up to then have been wearing casual, modern T-shirts and tights, to go with the women's light, simple skirts and sleeveless dresses—begin to appear in ruffled shirts. The eighteenth century, banished since the opening number, is starting to seep back in. And now the male-female couple, as a unit, comes to the fore over the course of several segments: first in a sequence of antic duets performed at the front of a larger group, then in an acrobatic, dramatic couple dance where only one man and one woman occupy the stage, followed in turn by a more romantic pas de deux, a slower dance in which each step or gesture, each bend of the knee in an articulated arabesque, marks a beat in the music.

At the end of this variation, the man remains alone onstage, caught in a Petrouchka-style droop. When he begins to move, it is with a series of sharp, agonistic movements of the hands and arms that gradually progress to his feet. Eventually this develops into a delightful, full-bodied, virtuosic solo, before he collapses again into sagging stillness as the Bach variation comes to an end. As befits the puppet-like figure he is imitating, or inhabiting, the dancer seems animated entirely by the music.

Shortly after this singular male solo, and following another pas de deux that is even more romantic and tender than the earlier one, a new set of eight men and eight women fill the stage, and now we see that the women's clothes too have started to change, with firm bodices defining their upper bodies, sleeves covering their upper arms, and longer, tutu-ish skirts. The men, too, have traded their dark tights for knee-length britches. But when two additional couples enter midway through that sequence and perform in front of the assembled sixteen, those two women are still dressed in the older sleeveless, short-skirted mode—as if to suggest that the time periods, though starting to blur backward toward the eighteenth century, are still in flux.

And then comes the seeming finale, a glorious passage for twenty-eight dancers dressed in full eighteenth-century mode, with frogged jackets on the men and V-shaped bodices on the women: a dance so complicated that it appears to touch on everything that has come before, from full-circle celebration to male-female partnering to crossing, weaving diagonals and jointly coordinated high lifts. The fourteen couples form and re-form into trios, male-male duos, and various subsets of the whole. Square-dance formations and Russian-style foot-slaps give way to a full-group circle and then to concentric clusters, with the women grouped in the middle. As the piano music builds thrillingly to what sounds very much like an ending, the dancers cohere downstage in a finale-like pose: four tight lines facing the audience, with women lifted onto the shoulders of the back-row men while alternating rows of men and women stand or kneel in front of them. This galvanic, eminently picturesque moment is so satisfying that this time *everyone* in the audience applauds at its end.

And yet it is not the end, for even as the audience is still clapping, the music starts up again in a slow, quiet restatement of the initial theme, and all the dancers rise to perform a courtly dance together. Midway through the movement, they peel off to either side and are replaced by the dance's first couple, now dressed in modern clothes, who, in the last thirty seconds of the dance, move downstage from the back in a recognizable but slightly different recapitulation of their first duet. The circle has closed, and we have all arrived at the meeting point: of past and present, of Bach's music and Robbins's choreography, of everything that makes dance at its best eternally alive and yet hauntingly ephemeral.

The fact that Bach's music was so profoundly perfect, so complete in itself, was part of the challenge Robbins set himself in this work, and it was a challenge that sometimes daunted him. "It was like approaching a beautiful marble wall. I could get no toehold, no leverage inside that building," he told one interviewer shortly after finishing the work. "The first weeks of rehearsal were as if I were hitting it and falling down, and having to start over."

Nonetheless, the music itself is what ultimately underlay and supported everything he did. Hearing the Bach pianist Rosalyn Tureck perform the *Goldberg Variations*, Robbins commented that it felt like "a tremendous arc through a whole cycle of life . . . and then back to the beginning." It was this structure that, above all, guided his overall concept of the dance. He again used the arc metaphor in speaking with his friend Rosamond Bernier, years later, about this piece. "Mostly I feel that working on a ballet is knowing that there's an island out there which you've read about and heard about," he told Bernier in 1986,

> and you have to find your way to it, and once you get on it, you have to explore it. And by the time you've finished with the ballet, you've explored the island. And that, to me, is what music is. I don't always know how my ballets are going to end: I have to find that as I go along, it comes out of the steps or the choreography that I'm making. I do have a conception somewhere in the back of my head of the total arc of the music. I remember particularly feeling that about *The Goldberg Variations.*

By the time Robbins took up this task, Bach was already an old and much-loved acquaintance, and music in general was an integral part of his life. But it had always been that. As early as 1945, when he was in his twenties, Jerry was enough of a musical prodigy to compete in quiz-style musical games with the likes of Marc Blitzstein, Leonard Bernstein, and Adolph Green. His own cousin, a pianist named Robert Silverman, remembered how he and Jerry had sung part-songs to each other on the long drive from New York to Providence, tossing back and forth bits from Bach's *Two- and Three-Part Inventions*. "I'd give him the theme; he'd start, and I'd come in," Jerry's cousin recalled. "We also made up rounds; we harmonized." The word Silverman used to describe Robbins's musicality was "tremendous."

In fact, Robbins had been a pianist even before he had started to dance, as the review of his earliest public appearance confirmed. "A special feature of the evening, which had not been previously announced, was the playing of little Jerry Rabinowitz, son of Mr. and Mrs. Harry Rabinowitz of Weehawken," wrote a Jersey City paper in 1924, reviewing a local piano recital. "Little Jerry is only 6, and since the age of 3, has been composing and playing. Last evening, he played two of his own compositions, an 'Indian Dance' and a 'Russian Song.'" Both pieces, said the reviewer, were "typical of the music of the people for whom they were named, and showed a comprehension of music far beyond that of even most adults."

As his statement to Bernier about the "island out there" suggested, music was central to Robbins's conception of dance. This was true even in the one case where there was no music, his 1959 dance *Moves*, which he choreographed on his own company, Ballets: USA, for one of its earliest Spoleto appearances. A compelling, inventive, delicately emotional work, *Moves* is located (like so much else Robbins did) in the overlapping terrain between ballet and modern dance. Yet unlike any of his other dances, it is performed in complete silence. He had not intended this from the beginning; on the contrary, he was impatiently waiting for the commissioned score that Aaron Copland had promised to produce for him. "And he was late in writing it while I was already in rehearsal," Robbins remembered. "So I'd go to Aaron and he'd play me a piece of what he'd composed, and I'd leave for the rehearsal with some of the tunes and certainly the rhythm in my head. So I started to choreograph it, because there was no score, and I was doing that to counts." And then he decided the piece looked very interesting *without* the music, so he choreographed the whole ballet in silence. It proved to be a highly successful experiment—the dance is still revived in occasional New York City Ballet performances, and unlike some of the other work Robbins did for Ballets: USA, it is still interesting—but it was an experiment he never repeated, since he himself knew that music was at the heart of his enterprise. "The perimeter is the score," he said about his typical process of invention. "That holds you, as a form to get to your next moves, your next developments of what you want."

Because Bach's *Goldberg Variations* is such a mathematically precise, geometrically expansive piece of music—"very big and architectural," as Robbins put it—the choreography Robbins came up with had to be both grand and precise at once. In this he succeeded beyond anyone's wildest expectations. The dance is completely satisfying the first time you see it, and yet it is susceptible to repeated viewings, day after day or even hour after hour, each one yielding new perceptions, new revelations. In fact, *The Goldberg Variations* is so abundant, so profuse, that it seems to hold everything in its grasp: not just the world of the dance studio and the stage (as *Dances at a Gathering* seemed to do), but also the world of the court, the world of the pastoral couple, the civic world and the private world, the past and the present, so that men and women, ghosts and dreams, live bodies and remembered Baroque engravings, mingle to produce a vital, ever-transforming stage picture.

Complicated and wide-ranging as this seems, it all rests on a very narrow and specific base—the live performance by a single pianist. "They're depending on me to give them the cushion for when they're out onstage," commented Cameron Grant, one of the musicians who has played the *Goldberg* accompaniment for the New York City Ballet. Alluding to the Petrouchka-like male solo in the second half of the dance, he began to explain the role of the piano in that movement. "It starts with the man kind of drooped," he said.

"And then I hear Cameron start playing the music," interjected Tyler Angle, a young dancer who has performed that solo. "It's like the music happens and it's forcing him to pick up the hand—another note—pick up the other hand—another note—turn your foot out, you're not done yet. The male solo music brings the dancer to life."

To an audience member, the way the dance fits the music looks natural, even inevitable. Yet none of it was easy to come up with. For a long time, as Robbins said, it felt as if he was hitting a wall. This may have been exacerbated by complications in his personal life: by the time he started working on *Goldberg*, in the fall of 1969, he had been abandoned by Richard as well as Christine, and he was in a state of frequent despair. He was also taking drugs, including a dose of LSD that left him terrified and nearly suicidal. The psychoanalyst he was seeing in that period (Jerry was always seeing one psychoanalyst or another) actually wanted to hospitalize him, but he refused to go into a hospital and instead resorted to the usual cure, hard work.

A few days into his *Goldberg* rehearsals, however, he was forced to go to the hospital after all, because he'd snapped his Achilles tendon demonstrating a step to the dancers. The resulting six weeks in a wheelchair put him into a "terrible state" and a "DEEP DEPRESSION," as he wrote self-pityingly, and it would be months before he could move normally again. In this inhibited condition he couldn't face the complications of Bach, and instead he fell back on Chopin again, choreographing *In the Night*. Though he was finally able to return to his work on *Goldberg* in the spring of 1970, it seemed to take forever to finish—in part because he was again hospitalized, this time with hepatitis, in the final months of that year.

None of this angst is visible in the dance itself (unless the depth of feeling it evokes, even in the midst of its joyful pleasures, can be seen as an awareness of life's underlying dark side). Nor is any of it visible in the few minutes of rehearsal tape that were recorded in the studio around the middle of 1970. Here Robbins is rehearsing Patricia McBride and Helgi Tomasson in what would turn out to be their romantic pas de deux late in the second half, set to the poignantly slow Variation 25. The tape is silent, so one cannot hear the wonderful Bach music that brings this tender, almost melancholy duet to life. But even without the music you can get a strong sense of how Robbins worked with his dancers.

Quite frequently he would move in very close, as if he were

a third member of the entwined couple, reaching in between them to adjust McBride's torso or move Tomasson's arm. When he steps back to observe, he goes no farther than two or three feet away—and then, after watching them for a few moments with a warmly affectionate gaze, he steps in again. At one point he actually picks up McBride, demonstrating to Tomasson how to lift his partner with one arm, and then how to hold her. The Jerome Robbins shown in this tape is, at fifty-one, still very strong. He is also quite slender, and perhaps even more hand-some than in his youth. The silver beard that he first grew in his late forties (and was to keep for the rest of his life) conceals the slight goofiness of his smile, lending a dignified aura that matches his high, balding dome and his close-cropped silver hair. When he stands to demonstrate a step to his two young dancers, as they sit on the floor, he is agile and precise; then he returns to his chair by the mirror, watching them execute the move. Sometimes, as he murmurs instructions or moves one of their limbs from here to there, he smiles or even laughs with them, but for the most part his face is simply relaxed—calm yet completely attentive, with a look that is almost sleepy in his half-closed, thoughtful eyes. It is as if he is dreaming this piece into being, and is happy with his dream.

The *Goldberg Variations* premiered on May 27, 1971, and though it was received as a major work by critics and audience members alike, it did not win the uniform adulation *Dances at a Gathering* had garnered. Balanchine reportedly thought it was too long and homogenous (though Robbins did not hear this from him), but the most outspoken critique, and the one he definitely *did* hear, came from Arlene Croce, writing in *Ballet News*. "*Goldberg* is ninety minutes at hard labor," she began, and followed this up with: "When Robbins has wrestled every last musical repeat to the mat, we don't come away with a the-atrical experience but with an impression of ingenious musical visualizations." ("Ingenious" was her typical code word for attacking or even praising Robbins: it managed to imply that he was simply a master tinkerer, a shyster mechanic who was somehow able to get his faulty engine running through the clever insertion of a bobby pin.) She objected to the whole ballet—which she insisted "doesn't really exist as a ballet"—on the grounds that it lacked any kind of overarching idea or conception that could offer us a new image, a new experience, even as she also complained that "The business of the dancers' switching from twentieth- to eighteenth-century drag or vice versa is just a scholastic platitude—'Bach Our Contemporary.'" That this might actually represent an overarching idea, though one with which she lacked sympathy, did not seem to matter to her. But like the strong critic she was, she eventually unearthed the essential point even as she remained deaf to its charm. "In *Goldberg*," she observed,

> the canvas is large and crowded; we lose the individual in the mass, and I presume that loss is intentional. The emphasis may fall on anyone; a corps member may shine like a star. In a way, *Goldberg* improves upon Paul Draper's method of democratizing Bach's music by tap-dancing to it—it makes Bach a vast sounding board for a collective morale, and though I find the morale sticky, it gives me something to look at. (I'm speaking of the first part of the ballet; the second part, which is like a week in a suburban domestic-relations court, puts me to sleep.)

That last line was typical of Croce's destructive wit, a quality that charmed her fans while making her victims tremble with anger and distress. But still nastier, to the choreographer's ears, would have been her comparison between his carefully-worked-out ballet steps and Draper's tap-dancing—yet another way of suggesting to her readers that Jerome Robbins had never transcended his origins as a Broadway hoofer.

There were times when Robbins took the critics' objections to heart (as he did, say, with Walter Kerr's critique of *Fiddler on the Roof*, which touched a nerve precisely because it coincided with Jerry's own doubts about the production). But in this case, although Robbins adjusted *The Goldberg Variations* in minor ways over the next few years, cutting out one brief dance sequence and slightly altering others, he never adopted Croce's view as his own. Perhaps he was buoyed by the praise of musicians such as Rosalyn Tureck, who assured him, "I am more deeply impressed than ever with your extraordinary sensitivity to musical structure and your genius in creating the transfer to the visual and communicative gesture." In any event, Robbins was later to describe *Goldberg* as the work of which he was most proud.

Nor did Croce's scathing remarks cause him to give up on his beloved Bach. He did not return immediately to this source, as he had with Chopin after *Dances at a Gathering* (and perhaps that pause was a good thing, in that it enabled the source to refresh itself). But in the 1990s, when he was in his seventies, Robbins made three dances based on the music of Johann Sebastian Bach: two for the New York City Ballet, and one for Mikhail Baryshnikov, who had recently formed his own dance group.

The ballet *2 and 3 Part Inventions*, set to the music of that name, was initially devised for students at the School of American Ballet, and they performed it in June of 1994. Six months later, the New York City Ballet took it up and gave it a professional premiere, and the piece has remained part of the NYCB repertory ever since. It features eight dancers—four men, four women—performing to twelve separate pieces of solo piano music. Like the score to which it is set, the dance is noteworthy for its frequent use of canon, with each dancer picking up in turn what the previous dancer has done; it also features a number of delightful couple dances (including one for two men, and another for two women). There is an underlying sense of lightheartedness or wit, and the dancing is often beautiful, but in comparison to *Goldberg* it is definitely a minor work. In part, perhaps, because it was devised for students, the steps seem more limited in scope than they did in that earlier masterpiece: they adhere more slavishly to the music, and to ballet tradition, rather than attempting to erase boundaries, as Robbins had done in 1971. The ending—where the eight dancers slowly exit, taking their bows as they go and leaving one woman alone onstage—feels somewhat low-key, like the ending of *Dances at a Gathering*, rather than gloriously show-stopping, like the end of *Goldberg*. It does not in any way seem that Bach has failed Robbins here, and if you had never seen *The Goldberg Variations*, you would find this piece perfectly delightful. It just feels a bit small and tidy, after that experience of marvelous expansiveness.

The same might be said of the 1997 *Brandenburg*, though it is a larger and more ambitious work than the *Inventions*. Instead of four couples, it features up to nine, arranged in various ways over the course of the forty-five-minute dance; and instead of a single piano, it employs the full orchestra. The music is of course gorgeous (it includes parts or all of four of the six Brandenburg concertos), and the dancing often is too, especially in the full-scale, constantly changing sequence set to the final Allegro of Brandenburg #3. Here the novelty and excitement of the mingled ballet and folk gestures, not to mention the brilliant deployment of eighteen dancers at once in circles, reels, interwoven lines, and other figures, at times echo the grandeur of *Goldberg*. But whereas the earlier dance emphasized oddness and weirdness—a soloist facing a group, four women dancing with three men, complicated counterpoint in place of simple canon—*Brandenburg* relies almost entirely on male-female couples in regular formation, often dancing in unison.

Yet if it lacks the depth and breadth of *The Goldberg Varia-*

tions, it is still a pleasure to watch, in part because the dancers themselves are obviously finding so much joy in it. Emily Coates, who was part of the group on whom Robbins choreographed the dance over the course of nearly two years, recalled what it was like to learn and dance "the last new creation he made." She remembered that in addition to the principals— Wendy Whelan, Jock Soto, Lourdes Lopez, and so on—the cast included "the young cohort I was with . . . Chris Wheeldon, Benjamin Millepied, me, Samantha Allen . . . and it really felt like he was shaping *us* to be Robbins dancers." What he cared most about, she said, was not technique, but feeling. "It was like: Lose the focus on technique, please, people. You have the technique. Please be human," Coates noted. "He very rarely gave a technical correction—would you please turn out more, your toe's not pointing. It was: The music is doing this, and can you do this. And: how do you take someone's hand? Are you looking at them? Where are you looking? All those details were important to him."

As opposed to *West Side Story Suite*, a late work in which she also participated, "*Brandenburg* was a more searching process," she recalled, and it required a great deal of rehearsal time, involving a substantial amount of trial and error. But amid the searching there was still room for fun, and for gentle divergences from the standard classical style. "There were lifts when we were lifted by our boys, but a lot of it was very playful—kids at play. And we were doing the same movements" as the boys, remembered Coates. She recalled with gratitude how Robbins, if he liked and respected you as a dancer, would adapt his choreography to your abilities. "In *Brandenburg*, for instance, he made a quartet that was me, Benjamin, Chris Wheeldon, and Samantha Allen, and he wanted us to cartwheel," she said. "I could not, for the life of me, cartwheel on the left. And he changed it! He said, That's okay, we'll cartwheel on the right."

In Emily Coates's view, Bach's music offered Robbins something special to build on. "A score like *West Side Story* drives the story with every note," she pointed out. "But Bach did something different for Jerry. Bach gave him a firm formal foundation to support his more lyrical movement. It lent him a greater degree of architectural support." And if Bach affected Robbins, she felt, Robbins also affected Bach. He "rode Bach's theatrical impulses and altered them for his needs. The opening he choreographed for *Brandenburg*, for example, rides the tone and tempo of the music. It begins in a circle, with a joyful, playful dance for us, the younger dancers. The idea of youth comes out of the energy of the piece, but Jerry also added and accentuated this feeling through the choreography and his choice of who was dancing. . . . Bach is like theatrical clay for him," Coates concluded, "sturdy enough to support really different scenarios but also malleable in his hands."

It was in *Suite of Dances*, the 1994 piece he made specifically for and with Mikhail Baryshnikov, that Robbins truly showed how malleable Bach could be. A dance first performed as a season-opener for Baryshnikov's newly created White Oak Dance Project, this solo work (a rarity in Robbins's oeuvre) was built on individual segments from Bach's Six Suites for Unaccompanied Cello. Initially Robbins developed five dances to five discrete movements: the Prelude from Suite #1, the Gavotte from Suite #5, the Sarabande from Suite #5, the Prelude from Suite #6, and the Gigue from Suite #1. Less than two months before the premiere, he decided to drop the Gavotte, finalizing *Suite of Dances* as a four-movement piece. But that was only the last in a series of inspirations and alterations that had taken nearly two years from start to finish.

From 1992 to 1994, the seventy-something Robbins and the forty-something Baryshnikov worked intermittently together in the studio, usually to music provided by a rehearsal pianist, though very occasionally to taped cello music. (The live cellist,

Wendy Sutter, only showed up shortly before the end, joining them in January of 1994.) In the earliest of the rehearsals
captured on tape, the two men frequently dance side-by-side,
with the choreographer marking the precise steps and weight
shifts and torso movements, and the dancer turning them into
dance. This is a noticeably older Robbins than the one in the
1970 *Goldberg* tape. Though he can keep the beat exactly, he
tends to shuffle rather than actively picking up his feet, and his
straight-backed torso is now marked by a bit of a belly. But he
is still able to give Baryshnikov all the necessary cues by demonstrating them.

There is something wonderful in the sight of the two of
them together, the older man lumbering but confident, the other
moving lightly but a bit uncertainly, always with his eye on his
instructor. Baryshnikov is obviously the better dancer, but Robbins possesses gravitas and brains—though Baryshnikov is no
dope, as his occasional questions and observations make clear.
And this dancerly intelligence in turn feeds into Robbins's
method. ("When he saw focus, effort to understand, effort to
really be in conversation with him and what he wanted—and
intelligence—he was very respectful," Emily Coates remarked
of the Jerome Robbins of this period. "I would say—I'm just
thinking of the dancers he preferred—they were all extremely
articulate in all sorts of ways, including verbally. And then it
became a conversation of equals with him.") The feeling generated by the two men in the studio is reminiscent of a highly
moving passage in Mark Morris's *Hard Nut*, where the older
Drosselmeier is introducing the youthful Nutcracker to the
world—except that in this case the world that Robbins is showing Baryshnikov is not the wider world of all possible experience, but his own interior world, his own inner life. And unlike
the two men in the Mark Morris dance (for that matter, unlike the three people in the *Goldberg* rehearsal tape), these two
never touch. Yet there is a constant sense of connection be-

tween them, a continuous sense of manifestly *physical* thinking that is being transmitted from an aging, hampered body
to a younger, perfect one. At times, as he stands and watches
Baryshnikov throwing himself wholeheartedly into the complicated steps, the approving Robbins vaguely gestures with
his own arms—not to demonstrate anything, but purely in response to the music, like a conductor who unconsciously sings
along with his orchestra.

At a much later rehearsal of the same project, held in December of 1993, Robbins was joined by Jennifer Tipton, who
had been his lighting designer since the late 1950s, and Santo
Loquasto, the production and costume designer for this dance.
In the recording made on this occasion, the two new observ-
ers are mainly silent; what conversation there is takes place
between the choreographer and his dancer. "Misha, if it's too
slow, say so," Robbins says of the pianist's pace, and later, after
the first dance has been completed and Baryshnikov is noticeably panting: "Yeah, yeah, catch your breath." The choreography has reached a much more final shape now, with a lot of
expressive arm gestures suggesting struggle or angst, and a certain number of Russian-style and even Hasidic-looking steps.
There are moments of evident comedy (Baryshnikov pulling
himself up from the floor by the scruff of his neck), but the
overall feeling of the piece leans toward the weighty, even the
nightmarish. The long final dance to the Gigue, for instance,
involves a relentless progression back and forth along a straight
line, with the dancer moving repeatedly from the far end of the
studio to the near one and then back again, as if he were caught
in a narrow tunnel from which he only manages to break out at
the end.

The whole *Suite*'s gestural vocabulary seems to derive as
much from modern dance as from ballet, but it pays tribute to
Baryshnikov's pyrotechnic skills as a ballet soloist, and there is
still the sense, even at this late date, of a master craftsman play-

ing with a wonderful new toy. How, exactly, can he exploit this body's capacity to do just about anything? What human feelings can it evoke? How casual can it seem? How funny? How Russian? How sexy? And how long can it keep up a sense of perpetual motion? Particularly in one segment (the Sarabande from Suite #5), every element of Baryshnikov's dance character, from light and witty to soaring and precise, seems to come into play. "That's a good one," Baryshnikov says breathlessly when he finishes, and Robbins agrees: "It's a keeper."

The world premiere of *Suite of Dances* took place at the New York State Theater on March 3, 1994, at the opening of White Oak's new season. As the curtain rose, the solo cellist and the solo dancer were both already onstage, she standing and looking down at him, he sitting with his back to the audience, looking up at her, with his arms reaching back to prop up his body, one leg stretched out in front of him. Something of the studio's relaxed feeling has been carried over here (not least in terms of costuming, for Loquasto has copied the red warm-up outfit Baryshnikov was wearing the day he attended rehearsals), and this opening allows one to imagine that in a sudden impulse of performative enthusiasm, the two of them have decided to play and dance to this music they know so well.

After she seats herself on the lefthand side of the stage, the cellist's first note and the dancer's first gesture seem to emerge simultaneously—though if you look closely, you can see that Baryshnikov is subtly cuing the beginning of each section. He manages to suggest, in this first dance to the first Prelude, that he is inventing the steps as he goes along, improvising to music he knows extraordinarily well—and that sense of personal possession of the material continues throughout the performance. The pyrotechnic Sarabande is a great success, provoking audience laughter with the scruff-of-the-neck gesture; the later Prelude, though perhaps overly filled with melodramatic psychologizing, works just fine in Baryshnikov's rendition. Perhaps most surprising, in this staged version, is the back-and-forth tunnel-dance with which Robbins closes the circle, returning us to the Gigue of Suite #1. In the studio, this final segment felt claustrophobic, constrained, excessively repetitious; here on a wider stage, the little dancing figure seems more sympathetic, more animated, and when he finally bursts out of his trammeled path and covers the whole available space with his leaps and turns, the transformation is thrilling. When he stops, the *Suite* has clearly reached its end, and the audience goes wild.

It would have been wonderful to be there and see this live: to watch the brilliant performance, and then to see the proudly smiling choreographer join the dancer and the musician onstage, holding hands as they all three took their bows. But *Suite of Dances*, though it succeeded beautifully on that occasion, was not destined to be one of Robbins's greatest works. It depended too heavily on the strength and the glamor of its originating dancer, perhaps leading the choreographer to underestimate the amount of work *he* needed to do. Too few of the gestures and patterns were inherently interesting, and there was a kind of literalness in the translation of notes to steps: skipping to the music's skippy parts, hands flung side-to-side on the cello's long, loud strokes. If the performer had merely been a typically good dancer, Robbins might have spotted these shortcomings, but Baryshnikov's overwhelming charisma and skill were enough to disguise these flaws, or at least make Robbins believe they were unimportant.

And then there was the problem of the dance's excessive interiority. It must have been a terrible temptation for Robbins, to have this singular dancer at his disposal, this marvelous solo performer available to him as a kind of second self. The natural impulse, given such an instrument, would have been to investigate through dance the choreographer's own inner life— his persistent angst, his saving sense of humor, his complicated sexuality, and, not least, his lifelong desire to break out of preset pathways, combined with his nearly overwhelming fear of doing so. And the individual voice of the cello, so human in its tones, must also have seemed conducive to such thoughts. It is not at all surprising that Robbins gave in to the temptation.

But to use Bach for these purposes was to betray what Bach had given him at his best: a sense of the intense communality of dance and music, in time and over time, as a collective, boundary-crossing event. *Suite of Dances* is a lovely tribute to its original cast member, a commemoration of a particular dance moment, somewhat in the vein of *Dances at a Gathering*. But Robbins's *Goldberg Variations*, like the music from which it derived, is an abundant, irreducible gift to all of us.

In Memory Of . . .

IT HAD REACHED the point where people were beginning to die around him. The idea was becoming personal. He himself had long since passed sixty; seventy loomed in the near distance. His body was no longer the flexible, easy instrument he had depended on in his youth. Besides his hospitalizations for the torn Achilles tendon in 1969 and hepatitis in 1970, he had been forced to undergo surgery for diverticulitis in 1977. Mortality was encroaching, and his level of anxiety, too, was increasing. After one particularly stressful period in 1975—during which he discovered that his latest lover was involved with someone else, at the same time as he was losing his beloved Snedens Landing place, since the landlords had turned down his offer to buy—Jerry went so far as to commit himself in early summer to McLean's mental hospital. Even after he emerged three weeks later, he still felt shaky, and it was months before he could really work again.

Still, the decade and a half that encompassed the period between his celebratory *Goldberg Variations* and his death-ridden
In Memory Of . . . contained numerous professional satisfac-
tions. In 1975 Robbins contributed five ballets to Balanchine's
Ravel festival—including the substantial *In G Major*, starring
the recently returned Suzanne Farrell—and in 1981 he created
two more works for the Tchaikovsky festival, despite his lack
of enthusiasm for that particular composer. The discipline itself, Robbins acknowledged, was worth something. "Whenever we did our festivals that Mr. Balanchine organized, suddenly we were all doing Stravinsky ballets or Tchaikovsky
ballets or Ravel ballets, whether we thought we wanted to or
not," he once commented. "And that wasn't a bad discipline. It
sometimes is good to work not where you always feel the most
comfortable or the most ready." He also noticed a corollary,
that "the days when I *do not* want to go to the theater, and *do
not* want to choreograph, because I don't know what I'm doing
and I'm the most upset about it, is the day when something
happens." In short, a choreographer could not afford to be an
overly sensitive prima donna—among other reasons, because
rehearsal rooms and dancers might not be available at his preferred times. "Terpsichore has to come down between three
and six on a Friday afternoon, even though you may feel better
between ten and twelve," Jerry wryly observed.

In addition to his collaborative work at the New York City
Ballet, this period marked significant acknowledgment of Robbins's stature as an individual choreographer. In December of
1981 he was awarded a medal of honor at the Kennedy Center
(where his fellow honorees included Cary Grant, Helen Hayes,
Rudolf Serkin, and Count Basie). Earlier that year, in September, he had taken a group of NYCB dancers on a groundbreak-
ing tour of China. Because Balanchine hadn't wanted to have
anything to do with the China escapade, the group of fourteen

dancers traveled to Beijing, Shanghai, and Canton under the label "Jerome Robbins Chamber Dance Company."

His personal life also seemed to be entering a new phase involving longer and more stable relationships with men. In 1976 he met the darkly handsome photographer Jesse Gerstein (then only nineteen years old), and the two remained a couple for many years, traveling to Europe and the Caribbean together as well as enjoying each other's companionship at home; even after they officially broke up, in the 1980s, they remained close friends. By 1984 Jerry had fallen in love again, this time with a young man named Brian Meehan, with whom he carried on an affair into the 1990s. He also settled the problem of summer rentals by buying his own summer house in Bridgehampton in October of 1979. And though he occasionally toyed with possible plays and other Broadway projects, he ultimately remained faithful to the New York City Ballet, contributing one or two new dances during most of its annual seasons and at the very least restaging his old ballets on new dancers.

Yet he could not but be aware of the near presence of death. His father, Harry Robbins, died in December of 1977, and his aunt Mary, of whom he had been fond, died the following April. Meanwhile, his close friend Dan Stern, who was younger than Jerry, had been hospitalized with a heart attack in late 1977, and though he survived, it was worrisome. Another source of anxiety was Balanchine's first heart attack, which occurred in the spring of 1978; it was followed in 1979 by a bypass operation, which necessitated such a prolonged absence from the NYCB that Jerry had to finish Balanchine's *Le Bourgeois Gentilhomme* dance for him. By 1982 Balanchine's generally weakened condition (he was suffering from Creutzfeldt-Jakob disease, a degenerative brain disorder) had become so obvious to the company that its board and staff were beginning to talk privately and in some cases publicly about the question of succession. Then, on December 2, 1982, Jerry suffered a more private loss, when his beloved secretary, Edith Weissman, died of a heart condition. She had only become aware of her illness during the previous summer, so there had not been much time to prepare, either mentally or practically. When she died, Jerry was holding her hand: "It's left a hole in the galaxy," he noted in his journal.

So when George Balanchine died on April 30, 1983, it must have seemed to Robbins that fate was piling loss upon loss. Yet instead of being plunged into despair, he became more active than ever. When Balanchine died, he was already at work on two new dances: *Glass Pieces* (choreographed to the music of Philip Glass) and *I'm Old Fashioned* (based on the dance moves of Fred Astaire, and set to music by Morton Gould). Neither represents his finest work, but each is memorable in its own way, and they are very different from each other. Both new dances premiered in the spring of 1983.

Meanwhile, in the period leading up to and immediately following Balanchine's death, Robbins was immersed in the internecine squabble over the command of the New York City Ballet. Certain board members argued that Balanchine had wanted the company left in the hands of Peter Martins, possibly in order to prevent Lincoln Kirstein from controlling it. Kirstein, by contrast, argued that Balanchine had left no succession plans whatsoever, and that he himself should be both artistic director and general director. Both plans excluded Jerome Robbins from any title implying directorship, reducing him to the level of one of several company-associated "ballet-masters." Robbins had a fit and resigned. The board and Martins urged him to come back, and the final arrangement they worked out had Peter Martins and Jerome Robbins holding equal status, running the company together. In practice what this meant was that the administrative tasks generally fell to Martins while Robbins focused more on his own ballets—but at least the NYCB had been preserved, and with its legacy as Balanchine's own company intact. Everyone understood that Jerry was a major part of that legacy, and they worked hard to keep him happy, allowing him more rehearsal time and a better choice of dancers than anyone else was given.

The first piece he created that really made use of this new freedom was *Antique Epigraphs,* which premiered in February of 1984. Choreographed for eight women and drawing on postures derived to a certain extent from classical Greek art, the dance managed to be about the past without being explicitly about death. Its primary impulse came from the music, a score by Debussy called *Six épigraphes antiques* that was based on some fake-classical poems actually written by a contemporary Frenchman named Pierre Louÿs. It was a score Jerry had already used once, in 1952, when it provided the music for a dance he titled *Ballade.* Never satisfied with the lukewarm response that had greeted that earlier dance, Robbins happened to be listening to the music three decades later and thought, "Gee, I'd like to try this again." This time, he resolved, he would create something that stayed closer to the roots of the music's Greek-inspired source. (The earlier dance had pursued the curious question of what happens to various roles—Petrouchka, Giselle, Hamlet, Traviata—when they're not being performed but "just sort of hanging around somewhere," as Jerry put it, "waiting for an actor or singer or dancer to come in and bring them to life again": an interesting idea, though perhaps not one easily susceptible to dance presentation.) And this time he would focus entirely on the female form, embodied in such NYCB dancers as Kyra Nichols and Maria Calegari.

Though the dancers wear flowing classical-style costumes, with high Empire waists and long, transparent skirts, the finished dance stems from many apparent sources besides ancient Greece. Renaissance paintings of the Graces, for instance, seem to lie behind the trio of dancers who intertwine their arms together as the other five women watch. And there are other influences too: the score itself, which goes from Egyptian-sounding flute music to American Indian–style droning passages, evokes a range of dance cultures that are not necessarily Hellenistic. But by the dance's closing moments, when all eight dancers line up in a row, taking various different poses and then freezing (or "friezing") into position at the end, we are strongly reminded of Greek statues. And in fact this turns out to be the source of those gestures, though it was not a source Robbins had recognized until he was almost finished.

"I started the ballet," he told an interviewer a couple of years later, "and it was only when I got near the end of it I realized one of the things that was haunting me were statues in Naples at the National Museum. Many, many years ago I'd walked into a room and there were four or five bronze statues, life-sized statues of women with enamel eyes, who were still." Robbins recalled finding their concentration on him "alarming, almost" ("it was like walking into the middle of a ritual with these people around you"), but he also wanted to capture that sense of concentration, so "near the end of the ballet, I turned my dancers, more or less, into those statues."

Robbins was using this story to illustrate the way in which a choreographer can never fully understand what is motivating him. "That's why when you say, *Do I know the form?* or *Was this the influence?*, I don't think that any choreographer can tell you that. I mean, they may say, *Oh, this or that, here, there*, but really our work is composed of all our experiences, which are conscious or unconscious, and come out that way. And besides," Robbins continued, "dance is so abstract, non-verbal, non-analytical, that you can't put your finger on it. . . . This is a magical ritual of an abstract kind which is a fantasy, and puts you in a place which no other theatrical experience can give you."

If the unconscious sources of a ballet were part of the point, for Robbins, then so was the possibility of returning to

music that had once meant one thing and now meant something completely different. This exact experience, which he
had undergone with Debussy's *Six épigraphes antiques*, struck him
even more forcefully when he came upon Alban Berg's Violin
Concerto less than a year later. "When I found a recording
of the Berg," he said, "I was so intensely moved by it. And a
friend of mine pointed out that I'd heard it with him, three or
four years earlier, and although it had struck me, it didn't stay
with me enough to have to do it. But at the time I was ready
for it—to be able to deal with it, or be sensitive enough to deal
with it—it was many, many years later." What had happened,
between that first hearing in, say, 1980 and the later one in 1983
or 1984, was the occurrence of a number of deaths that had affected him personally. And what came out of it was the dance
In Memory Of . . .

For Robbins, that ellipsis was important. He did not want
to specify anyone in particular to whom this dance was dedicated, because it was meant to apply to *all* the deaths, the recent
ones and the ones from other times and places: Weissman's and
Balanchine's, his father's and his mother's and his aunt's, not to
mention the prospect of his own. It was also meant to apply to
other losses, such as Tanny's terrible illness—the same illness,
polio, that killed the eighteen-year-old girl, Manon Gropius,
in memory of whom Berg initially wrote his Violin Concerto.
And then there were all the AIDS-related deaths and illnesses
that, since about 1981 or 1982, were increasingly afflicting those
in Jerry's world. (The Jerome Robbins Foundation, which he
had set up back in 1959 to share some of his wealth, began
around this time to devote a large share of its resources to helping dancers with AIDS.) So it was crucial to him that the dance
"should not be connected to one person, but to the sense of
losing people and the struggles that they go through when they
are ill and die, and hopefully arrive at peace for themselves." In

other words, it was *not* just a dance about Balanchine's death, despite the critics' evident desire to see it that way.

Perhaps they took this line, in part, because Robbins had employed Balanchine's own prima ballerina, Suzanne Farrell, to dance the role of the young girl who struggles with and is transfigured by her death. But none of this—neither the casting of Farrell nor the central involvement of a figure representing Death—was a part of Jerry's initial vision. It was the music which had spoken so strongly to him, and it was the music alone which motivated the first-movement segment, in which a man and a woman danced together against the background of eight other couples. In keeping with the somber, erratic music, this opening section was dark and anxious, but also dreamlike and strange. It possessed its own kind of romantic, even tender moments, such as the one where the man picked up the woman and rocked her in his arms—though not like a baby, for she was stretched out and facing downward, her hands covering her face, rather than comfortably cuddled.

The score was extremely complicated, with symbolic numbers and people's initials woven into the music in a way that meant something specific to Berg but not, quite likely, to any casual listener. Jerry was as far as one could be from a casual listener. He listened to the music obsessively, and he also studied everything about Alban Berg's story, including Berg's affectionate relationship with Manon, the young daughter of Alma Mahler; his grief at her sudden death, and his abandonment of the opera *Lulu* to write this concerto in her memory; his use of twelve-tone music as well as a peculiar numerical code (with 23, for instance, standing for male and 10 standing for female); Berg's own terminal illness, and his increasing despair in the Nazi-run Austria of 1935; and his love affairs, at least one of which produced an illegitimate child. Holding all this in his mind, but in particular paying attention to the vagaries of the music, which he knew bar by bar, Robbins faithfully followed the score, creating steps to all its odd measures—until, suddenly, it dropped him cold.

"I'd gotten that far, and I didn't know how to use the rest of the music," he told Rosamond Bernier. "I got very depressed, because the music is depressing, the subject is depressing. And I wasn't happy with what I'd made so far. But by chance—as that happens—Adam Lüders was present at that rehearsal. And I dismissed everyone else, thinking, I'm going to stop the ballet here. And I said, 'Well, I've still got a half-hour; let me see. Come on, Adam,' and I started working on the pas de deux. I didn't know I was going to use that music as a pas de deux until that moment."

"You saw him suddenly as the Death figure," Bernier prompted.

"Yes," Robbins answered her. "I hadn't figured on that before. I didn't know whether I was going to use a large group in this section; I didn't know how I was going to use it. But when I saw him I thought: Well, let me try this. And as soon as I started it was like the doors opened for me . . . It was almost like automatic writing—it felt like I couldn't make a mistake."

For the next rehearsal of the pas de deux, he called in Suzanne Farrell, and the experience of the two dancers working together seemed to be as miraculous as his own. "We all fused in an extraordinary way," said Jerry. "I've never had a rehearsal like that, where it was almost as if it had already been done. No matter what I asked them to do, it led immediately to the next thing, and that section was done and we moved on to the next." The entire duet was completed in only two rehearsals, an unheard-of achievement for Robbins, who could take weeks or even months working on a ten-minute segment. "It was rather hair-raising," he told Bernier, "and I think some of that quality you'll see in the performance of it."

He's right. Even if you know nothing of Alban Berg and his sadness about the dead girl—even if you don't know there *is* a

dead girl behind this music—you can see in the dance between
Adam Lüders and Suzanne Farrell a young woman resisting
and then submitting to death. This whole segment, in which
the solo violin dominates the music, often in a high, keening
voice, is more fierce and agonistic than anything that has come
before; in dance terms, it is also far more original.

It begins with a young woman—the same young woman
who was part of that first couple—now kneeling onstage, facing us. Behind her stands a different man from the one she
danced with earlier, a new man whose movements are somehow more threatening, more overwhelming than those of her
previous partner. He pulls her up and into his grip, moving her
forward in a stiff-legged, side-to-side, rocking walk, as if she
were a child or a puppet. Like an abandoned puppet, she then
falls into a forward droop, body bent at the waist, arms hanging toward the floor, as he continues to dance alone, only to
resume his dance with her, now more frenzied and intense. At
one point, supporting her from behind, he releases her into a
high arabesque, her body in profile arching far backward and
raised up on toe. As she lets herself fall forward from this ver-
tiginous position—frighteningly, thrillingly—he swiftly moves
around to catch her from the front. He slides her along on the
floor, then scoops her up and rocks her in his arms. This time
the rocking is more like that of a parent with a curled-up child,
though a sense of discomfort is added to the apparent tenderness when she tilts her head back and stretches out her legs.
The man lifts her high above his head and lowers her to the
ground, at which point—in a gesture whose violence matches
the violence of the music—he drops her face-down on the
floor. She only lies there a moment before he pulls her abruptly
back into a sitting position, as if she were a rag-doll. Her body
remains frozen in this pose, but she is not completely still: she
turns her face away from him as he approaches her from the
right. Then he takes hold of her hand, and at this she appears

to collapse internally, her head and torso falling sideways toward him as he continues to pull on her. She lies there on the stage, seemingly lifeless, but when he picks her up and carries her offstage (this time very much like a child being cradled), she puts her arms around his neck.

This astonishing pas de deux may well be the high point of the dance, but its effect is magnified by the third and final segment, an eerie, magical passage in which the dancers are quite obviously ghosts. Three couples increase to four and then to eight, all doing strange, slow, repetitive movements that often involve standing on one leg and falling onto the other: a broken step, an awkward step, suggesting a discontinuity between the will and the body. As all sixteen ghosts stand together and sway their arms above their heads, like reeds in water, the original girl—this time in a white dress, with her dark hair long and loose around her face—emerges from behind them and begins to dance on her own. They form an open circle, their hands barely touching, and she runs around within it. And then, as the melancholy, terrifying music comes to its close, she is joined onstage by her two partners, the initial man and Death, who lift her body between them and proceed to carry her offstage, holding her upright as she extends her arms to either side and softly cycles her legs through the air that is beneath her.

Having made this nearly perfect and practically unrepeatable dance about death—so technically demanding that the company has only rarely been able to stage it in the years since, and so intense that it left the choreographer with little else to say on the subject—Robbins nonetheless returned twice more to the topic in the 1980s. Neither his *Quiet City* of 1986 nor his *Ives, Songs* of 1988 reaches the level of *In Memory Of*. . . , but he clearly felt impelled to continue for a time in an elegiac vein. *Quiet City*, a trio set to music by Aaron Copland, was dedicated to the memory of Joseph Duell, the dancer who had first taken on the role of Suzanne Farrell's partner in the opening movement of *In Memory Of . . .* In early 1986, less than nine months after *Memory*'s premiere, Duell killed himself by jumping out a window. Jerry, who had used the young man often in his dances but in this case had ultimately replaced him with Alexandre Proia, probably felt guilty as well as immensely sad.

As for *Ives, Songs*, it is a strange dance indeed, a kind of Agnes de Mille–meets–Dracula combination, in which small-town joys and pleasures are catalogued in numerous brief sequences that gradually move into a more pensive, mortality-confronting mood. The costuming (oversized hair ribbons and frilly dresses on the girls, knickers and dopey hats on the boys) does not help matters, but the real problem lies with the Charles Ives songs themselves, to which Robbins has been typically faithful. In their weird combination of upbeat, patriotic Americana and increasingly discordant sorrow, the score and lyrics convey a sense of unreality that the dance heightens rather than questions. The decision to place a "singer" figure onstage—not the actual baritone involved in the production, but a non-dancing male figure representing some kind of observer—further contributes to the dance's lack of direct feeling, its refraction of experience through an artistic lens. It was a noble experiment, perhaps (Robbins himself seemed quite fond of *Ives, Songs*), but the dance did not begin to achieve the felt intensity that characterized his more fully achieved *In Memory Of . . .*

By the 1990s, in any case, he apparently felt able at last to turn away from this darker material and resume his pleasurable dealings with Bach. First in *2 and 3 Part Inventions*, then in *Suite of Dances*, and finally in *Brandenburg*, he returned to the mood of an earlier self—not exactly the "sunny, funny" fellow Arlene Croce had asked for, but a person who was able to give and seek joy along with sorrow.

Robbins was now well into his seventies, and he was as

comfortable with himself as he was ever going to be. His popular reputation was secure (the 1989 *Jerome Robbins' Broadway*, a staged anthology of all his greatest hits, confirmed that), and so was his position at the New York City Ballet, where he was firmly ensconced as co-director and valued choreographer. He was also extremely well-off financially, in a way that few if any other choreographers had ever been. His net worth was over $5,000,000, and the sources of his income ranged from his annual paycheck at NYCB—a $100,000 salary, plus fees for each ballet—to his steady income from his musicals. (This amounted to $115,186 from *Fiddler* alone in the calendar year 1986, not to mention additional royalties every time *West Side Story*, *Peter Pan*, *Gypsy*, or any of the others was performed.) He also got paid a licensing fee for every ballet of his that was done by a non-NYCB company, at the rate of up to $25,000 per ballet. So even if he didn't feel particularly rich ("It was hard for him to spend money, especially on himself," commented his financial adviser, Allen Greenberg), he *was* rich, in a way that his own father could never have dreamed of.

Perhaps Jerry never did make peace with his youthful struggle against his parents: he was still fussing with his unperformable and indeed incompletable *The Poppa Piece* in 1992, fifteen years after Harry Rabinowitz had died. But in other ways Robbins managed to encompass his broken past and make it whole. He invited Jesse Gerstein, for instance, who had long since ceased to be his lover, to move back into his house in 1991, when Jesse was dying of AIDS, and Jerry took tender care of him for months. He took Jesse on trips—to Los Angeles, to Japan—when he was healthy enough, brought him to the Bridgehampton house over the summer, and hosted an intimate thirty-fourth birthday party for him over Labor Day. He also hired private nurses as Jesse got worse; and when he finally died on October 14, Jerry scattered his ashes on the beach at Bridgehampton. Meanwhile, he was also mourning his old friend Leonard Bernstein, who had died of lung cancer just a day before Jesse's death. "I felt a big piece of my life's construction had dropped away," he wrote to Lenny's children about their father's death.

But there was life in him still. Working with the young dancers at the New York City Ballet, it turned out, was both a way of escaping his growing sense of mortality and a way of confronting it. He wrote to a friend in November of 1995 about the *Brandenburg* rehearsals: "I can't show them what I want them to do so they all move around with stiff-legged movements imitating me and not my intentions. . . . It's such very hard work for me now. If I stay on my feet, my hips do not lock; it's when I sit down that I get stiff all over. The kids realize I'm not my old self and are trying to be helpful. They are a lovely bunch. I don't know how they remember all the changes I make all the time."

The kids, for their part, thought he was wonderful. They knew that Jerry had recently suffered a series of tiny strokes (transient ischemic attacks, the doctors called them); perhaps some of them had also heard about his prostate cancer and his heart problems. But from their point of view he could still do everything he needed to do as a choreographer. "He had a stroke in those years, which changed him," Emily Coates remembered. "But it did seem very much like when he came into the studio, any confusion he might experience out there in the world suddenly *whoosh*"—she collapsed her hands to demonstrate—"focused in. He knew how to be in the studio. He knew how to be looking at dancers, coaching movement, and making his work. He would come in, sit down—total focus, noticing everything—and then end the rehearsal and kind of wander out the Exit fire door. Yup. So that was Jerry in the last couple years of his life."

And though he could still get angry and seem over-sensitive about some things, he was also capable of great warmth and encouragement. "When he respected you, there was a sense you had a golden orb around you," said Coates. It was a chance for Jerry to be a new person, in a way, because these young people did not know the old one. "I mean, my feeling from the 1990s was—and perhaps because we were young and naive and didn't look back into history—he had no history with us, in terms of the McCarthy trials and so forth." And that meant that he could simply exist in the present with them, and perhaps even look toward the future. "He was really invested in shaping us and working with us. I found a very human man," Coates concluded.

By 1996, though, he was no longer going regularly into the studio. Friends noticed that he had memory lapses or fell asleep in the middle of things. But as late as the spring of 1998, he was still participating in the dance world. He attended rehearsals for a revival of *Les Noces* at the New York City Ballet, and he even came out for a curtain call at the May 20 performance. Perhaps he overdid it, for the morning after that evening performance, he felt so tired that he had to check into the hospital for ten days.

He could barely walk after that, but he still resisted using a wheelchair, still insisted on going to the beach house and visiting with friends. Brian Meehan, among others, took care of him, cooked for him, drove him to doctor visits. This went on for weeks amounting to months. On one such occasion in July of 1998, when Brian had just dropped him off, Jerry said to him, "Goodbye. God bless you." Brian, shocked because Jerry had never said this before, replied, "God bless you too."

That night, July 25, he had a massive stroke, and he never came out of the coma. Nadia Stern, Daniel's second wife, who was charged with carrying out his living will, insisted that the hospital release him, since he had wanted to die at home. And so it was there in the house on Eighty-First Street, on the night of July 29, 1998, surrounded by friends who were holding his hands as they softly played Bach recordings in the background, that Jerome Robbins died.

Coda

ANYBODY WHO REGULARLY, or even irregularly, attends dance performances in New York these days is bound to run across the name Jerome Robbins. The display corridor that adjoins the grand tier level of the City Center auditorium is named after him; so is the similar space on the main seating level of New York City Ballet's primary home at Lincoln Center. The largest performance space at the Baryshnikov Dance Center is called the Jerome Robbins Theater. The backstage area at the Brooklyn Academy of Music is the Jerome Robbins Green Room. And so on, throughout the city. Perhaps most noticeably, the public library's capacious repository of dance-related materials—a resource used by dance historians, dance critics, and amateur aficionados alike—is prominently labeled the Jerome Robbins Dance Division. The core of the holdings originally consisted of Jerry's own papers and recordings, but it has been augmented by gifts and purchases from other choreographers and dancers over the years. Robbins's initial bequest of $5,000,000 to underwrite the dance library made him, at that point, the largest individual donor the New York Public Library had ever had, and since he also specified that the Dance Division was to receive a fixed percentage of any future royalties from *Fiddler on the Roof,* a steady flow of income generated by his own work continues to support the Lincoln Center library.

Some of Robbins's current fame is undoubtedly the result of finances. He was one of the few choreographers ever to make a large amount of money, and by the time he died the estate was worth many millions of dollars (not to mention many more in future income from licensing and royalties). Besides generous bequests made to a series of friends, relatives, former lovers, and dance colleagues, he left a substantial portion of his wealth to the Jerome Robbins Foundation—an entity originally known as the Lena Robbins Foundation when Jerry founded it around the time of his mother's death, but renamed for the choreographer himself when it achieved nonprofit status in 1959. As of 2015, the foundation had assets of over $16,000,000, of which $1,396,966 was paid out in grants to various dance organizations, choreographers, and dancers during that calendar year alone. If you consider that something approaching this level of giving has prevailed during most of the two decades since Robbins's death, it does not seem surprising that his name is visible everywhere in the dance world.

But money alone does not account for his continuing reputation. In the past few years, *Fiddler on the Roof, On the Town,* and *The King and I* have all been revived on or near Broadway. *Gypsy* makes frequent reappearances there, and *West Side Story* is almost constantly in production somewhere, on the stages of high schools and amateur theatrical societies as well as on professional stages worldwide. Perhaps the average American does not know Jerome Robbins's name, but if you ask some of those average Americans—of just about any age—whether they have seen the movie *West Side Story*, they will almost invariably give you an emphatic yes. His influence lives on even where his name may not.

He has not been forgotten on the ballet stage, either. His own company, the New York City Ballet, will observe Jerome Robbins's centenary year in 2018 by putting on nineteen of his dances—a quantity that allows him to vie, for once, with Balanchine's role in the inherited repertoire. But even in a normal year the NYCB routinely revives his most popular works: the all-Robbins programs mounted in 2017, for instance, included *The Concert, Fancy Free, Glass Pieces,* and *Moves,* and previous seasons at Lincoln Center featured *The Goldberg Variations, West Side Story Suite,* and *NY Export: Opus Jazz.* *The Cage* has been performed by a variety of companies (most recently and unusually the Bolshoi Ballet in Russia) as well as with some frequency by the NYCB. Perhaps the most commonly loaned-out dance of them all is *Dances at a Gathering,* which often appears on the programs of ballet companies across America and abroad; it gets frequent revivals, for instance, at the San Francisco Ballet, which has been run for many years by the Robbins protégé Helgi Tomasson.

Yet a slight aura of the second-rate still infuses discussions of Robbins's ballet choreography. Arlene Croce's influence here has been deep and long-lasting, and even some of the younger dance critics will tell you that Robbins was great at Broadway productions but perhaps should have steered clear of ballet. This was not, incidentally, George Balanchine's view of the matter. His rationale for hiring and keeping Robbins alongside him at his own company came out in a remark he once made to Violette Verdy. "You know, Violette," Balanchine said to her, "the real American choreographer at the New York City Ballet is Jerry, not me. He's the one who can capture the fashions, the trends, the relaxed character of American dancers, their lack of a past or a style, but an ability to do all they're asked to do without discussion or preconception." And in the late 1960s, when Robbins was recalled to the City Ballet to contribute to the anniversary gala, Balanchine reportedly said to Patricia McBride, "You know, dear, you know why Jerry is here? Because he's *good.*" But Mr. B.'s expressed opinions apparently carry little weight among his own staunch admirers. They are determined to view Robbins purely in relation to the Master—as an unsuccessful, aspiring version of George Balanchine, a crass American lagging in the aristocratic Russian's wake—and as a result he is always found wanting.

Still, attention to Robbins's own choreography has continued to surface, and even to grow. Three enormous biographies of him appeared in the decade after his death, and two of them—Deborah Jowitt's *Jerome Robbins* and Amanda Vaill's *Somewhere*—were so thorough and intelligent as to render any other biographical investigation almost unnecessary. (Together, they have provided most of the factual basis for the present work.) Entire books have been written about *West Side Story* and *Fiddler on the Roof,* including scholarly cultural histories as well as blow-by-blow accounts of the way they were made. A remarkably good American Masters film about Robbins aired on television in 2009. A collection of his writings, edited by Amanda Vaill, is due out in 2018. There is no sign that he lacks adherents, or indeed committed fans. And yet a sense that he deserves to be celebrated for everything *other* than his ballets continues to prevail.

This is where I came in. When the Jewish Lives series at Yale University Press invited me to write a brief biography of Jerome Robbins, I was happy to oblige. I'd recently seen the movie of *West Side Story* once again, and on that basis alone I considered him a genius worth championing. I didn't know much about his ballets, but I was willing to learn, though I had a vague feeling that I would merely encounter a sub-Balanchine. I had, that is, unconsciously adopted the prevailing attitude espoused by the Croce-influenced dance critics (among whom I number several of my old friends).

Then I happened to see *The Goldberg Variations*. It was appearing on a 2015 program at the New York City Ballet, and though I was somewhat doubtful about the combination of Robbins and Bach (*What chutzpah!* I remember thinking), I wanted to see that particular program because it included a performance of *West Side Story Suite*. Little did I know. When *Goldberg* was over, I sat in my seat in a state of stunned amazement. I went back the very next week to see it again, and my gratitude for its abundance was even greater the second time. Above all, I couldn't get over the fact that this remarkable dance had been so effectively hidden away from me. I've been attending dance performances for my entire adulthood—a period which began at just about the time this work premiered, in 1971—and yet until that moment I had never seen *The Goldberg Variations*, never even heard a word about it.

Of course, it takes a major ballet company to put it on, one with a very deep, strong corps as well as enormously talented soloists. Obviously not every season can accommodate an eighty-minute piece involving thirty dancers. Still, cost can't be a major factor. The New York City Ballet *has* the dancers, after all, and only needs to hire the one musician. There are no sets whatsoever, and the costumes, though evocative, are not at all elaborate. So why hadn't this brilliant piece of dance been appearing with some regularity at Lincoln Center?

I asked some dance-going friends about it, and the ones who had seen *The Goldberg Variations*—mainly way back in the Seventies—remembered liking it a great deal. But some of them also recalled feeling slightly abashed about their affection, as if they had fallen for something rather louche. At first I attributed this simply to all the usual factors: Robbins's reputation as a Broadway song-and-dance man, his lower-on-the-totem-pole relation to the sainted Balanchine, etcetera, etcetera. But then, thanks in large part to Jowitt's and Vaill's biographies, I discovered the dirty truth. I learned that Arlene Croce had panned *The Goldberg Variations* when it first came out, as a result of which the dance-critic world—and possibly the NYCB itself—had devalued the dance ever since.

And it wasn't just *Goldberg*, I soon realized. Marvelous inventions abounded all throughout Robbins's career, from the delightful *Fancy Free*, the thrilling *Cage*, and the moving *Afternoon of a Faun* to the fetching *Antique Epigraphs* and the fantastic *In Memory Of*.... Some of them were occasionally trotted out, but where were the others in the regular NYCB repertoire? Why was *Dances at a Gathering* the only Robbins piece I routinely got to watch?

As I sat day after day and month after month in the booths of the Jerome Robbins Dance Division, viewing the recordings of these terrific dances over and over, I felt myself becoming something of a zealot. I was like a court-appointed lawyer who had initially accepted an assignment out of a general sense of justice but then discovered that her client was, amazingly enough, completely innocent. We would go to the wall on this one, I vowed: no plea bargaining for us! It became my sworn duty, as it were, to overturn the prevailing myth and establish the superiority of his ballets. Granted, Robbins did some great work on Broadway; no one who has seen *Peter Pan* or *West Side Story* can ever doubt that. But a lot of his musical-comedy work contains elements of coarseness, or sentimentality, or kitsch—qualities that are practically endemic to the genre—whereas the ballets are filled with a precise, deep-seated intelligence of a sort rarely credited to him.

It came down, I finally felt, to the issue of Robbins's narrative imagination. Abstraction ruled in the Balanchine era. It was one of the many gifts he brought to ballet, and his influence was justifiably powerful. But other kinds of dance ought to be able to coexist with abstraction if ballet as an art form is to thrive, and a choreographer like Jerome Robbins, who couldn't avoid a sense of drama even in his most abstract works, clearly brought something useful to the table. What is given to Robbins needn't be taken away from Balanchine; both kinds of choreography are needed if ballet is to remain healthy and alive.

And both kinds of choreography are capable of exhibiting all the subtlety and delicacy that dance at its best possesses. The fact that there is a narrative quality to Robbins's dances does not mean that people are meant to understand them completely. Despite their human or otherwise intelligible moments, his dances remain mysterious and multifaceted: Robbins is never simply giving us "clues" to his "meaning," any more than Balanchine is. And despite the critical attempt to separate Robbins's two kinds of achievement—to praise him as a Broadway hoofer or a brilliant script-doctor while downplaying the strength of his high-art choreography—such observations apply equally well to his finest musicals and his finest ballets. It is misleading to think that the existence of a script for *West Side Story* or the lack of a script for *The Goldberg Variations* somehow defines the meaning of either work. In neither case does the story supply the whole point, or even a large part of it. And in any case it makes no sense to ask what a given sequence in either production *means*, except perhaps in highly metaphorical and fanciful ways. The meanings are not fixed—they can change with the casting, or even with the viewer's mood— and they are not translatable into words, any more than Bach's or Bernstein's measures are. If there is meaning in these performances, it is emotional meaning, generally of a complicated and sometimes contradictory kind. That is what the narrative impulse produces, and that is what the grateful audience member recognizes each time: that she is as much a participant as the dancers or the actors or the musicians or the choreographer, because the emotional meaning resides in her.

Emily Coates, when asked to describe Robbins's influence on a younger generation of choreographers, had this to say about his connection to emotion: "Looking at Chris Wheeldon's work and Benjamin [Millepied]'s work and the work of the younger choreographers . . . the abstraction, that's from Balanchine—the energy, the technique, the reach, and the steps crafted directly to music. Jerry gives it heart. And I feel like when the work of my male peers has some heart, it's because they're being reminded of Jerry, an echo of Jerry."

This may well be true even when the influence is not fully acknowledged. Great contemporary choreographers like Alexei Ratmansky and Mark Morris naturally want to trace their ancestry back to Balanchine, and the tendency is therefore to leave the hierarchy in place. "Robbins wasn't nearly as good as Balanchine," Morris insists. "As far as great genius choreography, as far as choreo-musical absolute Bachian genius, Balanchine is unapproachable." And Ratmansky, at least in his public statements, has suggested an equal degree of admiration for his masterful Russian predecessor. Yet Ratmansky's own narrative imagination actually matches Jerome Robbins's in intensity if not in style, and though I have not spoken with him on the subject, I suspect he might acknowledge affinities between himself and the mid-century American. Even Mark Morris confesses to a certain degree of influence, though initially he could only come up with small points of comparison. "Well, our big rumble number in *Capeman* was of course the Dance at the Gym," Mark Morris mused, and he also admitted to stealing (and improving upon) "the piano ballet." But then he started to cast a wider net: "Stuff that I stole from Jerome Robbins. I can't think of anything except . . . well, observing. People observing other people dancing. It was just intimate and interesting to make a double point of view and make it—what is that called when you put the show within the show? . . . But also in Robbins and sometimes in my work it's not just people observing. It's like, come on, you knew you were going to dance. It's a dance show. It's like 'What? How did I find myself onstage?' I love that." And it is, in fact, that connection between the two realms—the notion that dance is a thing in itself and also a part of the rest of life, something real and something staged, simultaneously, with no barrier between the two—that marks both Robbins's and Morris's profoundest works.

"He's an inspiration, of course," Mikhail Baryshnikov said, speaking for the camera a few years after Jerome Robbins's death. "Very complex, and a wonderful man." Then he paused, and added softly: "I miss him."

It is tempting to leave that as the last word, but I want to bring back Robbins one last time and give *him* the final say. Because however tortured and angry and guilt-ridden he may have been, he was also extraordinarily aware—not only about his own character, but about the value of his dances and the importance of dance in general, particularly in terms of the way the art form was capable of acting upon its audience. And though he always spoke beautifully about his work, he also knew there was a time to be silent and let the work speak for itself. "Because there's no way of explaining dance, or all the ideas that go into a work," he told Rosamond Bernier, at the end of his hour-long taped conversation with her. "And although some of these things I've said may be helpful for an audience who hasn't seen our work to perceive them, still, it's best for them to hear what we say and put it away and respond to the work itself. Not try to always interpret it. I don't like things getting stamped with statements about them."

So the best thing you can do, right now or at some point in the near future, is to forget about everything I've said here and arrange to take a trip to the Jerome Robbins Dance Division at

Lincoln Center. There you will be able to watch his dances as he oversaw them, preserved in that congenial setting, where you can sit in your own booth and make up your own mind. The dance division is part of the public library, accessible with just a library card, which even out-of-towners can acquire for free. Anyone can make use of the collection. And everyone should.

All the passages in this book that are direct quotations are listed below in the order of their appearance, divided up by chapter headings; each quotation is identified by key words and then cited by source. Sources that are used frequently are abbreviated after the first use.

Epigraph

"It was . . . Rabinowitz": Deborah Jowitt, *Jerome Robbins: His Life, His Theater, His Dance.* New York: Simon & Schuster, 2004, p. 231. [Hereafter cited as Jowitt.]

Overture

"Mean as a snake": Helen Gallagher speaking in *Something to Dance About,* a 2009 American Masters film that aired on PBS. [Hereafter cited as PBS film.]

"I want you . . . audition . . . in my life": Amanda Vaill, *Some-*

where: The Life of Jerome Robbins. New York: Broadway Books, 2006, p. 279. [Hereafter cited as Vaill.]

"rehearsed it to death . . . Where do . . . dancer than that": Vaill, pp. 167, 326.

"I don't . . . was right . . . putting into it . . . different person": Vaill, pp. 371, 326.

"just murder . . . tormented": Vaill, p. 126.

"They used to . . . child abuse": Adam Phillips in conversation with the author.

"I stand . . . every one": Jowitt, p. 1.

"Hello . . . Dear Mommy . . . Jerry": Jowitt, p. 10.

"running . . . among them": Vaill, p. 28.

"Gerald Robbins": Vaill, p. 33.

"You better . . . with dancing": Vaill, p. 38.

"my first . . . theater people . . . little ballets": Vaill, pp. 45, 46.

"I was as . . . than anyone else": Jowitt, p. 32.

Fancy Free

"He picked . . . didn't go to": Jowitt, p. 50.

"little things": Vaill, p. 40.

"The Greatest . . . Ballet History!": Jowitt, p. 59.

"Have you ever . . . Last night," Vaill, p. 78.

"He would watch . . . believe in you": PBS film.

"I am . . . so many ways": Vaill, p. 82.

"badly painted . . . 'strange'": Jowitt, p. 64.

"His approach . . . portrayal": Jowitt, p. 64.

"I thought . . . they were doing": PBS film.

"That's it! . . . in mind!": Allen Shawn, *Leonard Bernstein: An American Musician.* New Haven: Yale University Press (Jewish Lives), 2014, p. 68. [Hereafter cited as Shawn.]

"There's a phrase . . . remove it": Jowitt, p. 83.

"real contact . . . he was interested": Jowitt, p. 44.

"Mexican": Shawn, p. 72.

"It was a surprise . . . I've ever done": Videotaped interview between Jerome Robbins and Rosamond Bernier, conducted at the New York State Theater and broadcast on WNET Great Performances on May 2, 1986. [Hereafter cited as Bernier interview.]

"Now the money . . . it's money": Sono Osato speaking in PBS film.

"laid a big egg": Vaill, p. 113.

"I make a disaster . . . will be over": Vaill, p. 114.

Age of Anxiety

"Tops in Terpsichore": Jowitt, p. 143.

"I wrote . . . wanted to dance": Jowitt, p. 144.

"My excuses . . . groin groans": W. H. Auden, *The Age of Anxiety: A Baroque Eclogue*. Princeton: Princeton University Press, 2011, p. 71.

"betrayed the Poppa . . . achieved, changed": Jowitt, p. 499.

"My deuce . . . private mental life": W. H. Auden, *The Age of Anxiety*, pp. 6, 4.

"quite as obscure . . . unassailable": Jowitt, p. 167.

"Dupes and . . . Communist Fronts": Shawn, p. 99.

"no one . . . at stake": Jowitt, p. 499.

"Tip to Red . . . Commies of all hues": Vaill, p. 193.

"stated . . . on 4/25/50": Jowitt, p. 191.

"friendly witness": Vaill, p. 215.

"I am going . . . much more . . . as an American": Vaill, p. 219.

"I'll never know . . . were a shit": Arthur Laurents speaking in PBS film.

"Stabbed by the wicked fairy": Vaill, p. 219.

"Hiya, loose lips!": Jowitt, p. 343.

"The Jew Piece": Jowitt, p. 423.

"You want to . . . Take him . . . One of the keenest . . . haunted me": Jowitt, p. 499.

"I accuse": Vaill, p. 193.

The King and I

"You are born . . . has *dignity*": Vaill, p. 183.

"It was . . . pushing the other": Vaill, p. 186.

"a stunning ballet . . . humor": Vaill, p. 187.
"Ballet is woman": Many sources, including Arlene Croce, "Balanchine Said," *The New Yorker,* January 26, 2009.
"When I watch . . . give up": Jowitt, p. 412.
"From the very beginning . . . There's a stage . . . really *about*": Jowitt, p. 144.
"He's so cool . . . like Balanchine": Jowitt, p. 314.
"eliminated almost . . . good manners": Vaill, p. 243.
"You are the only . . . work with": Vaill, p. 199.
"I fixed, but you changed": Jowitt, p. 277.
"a little wink . . . plotting together": Violette Verdy speaking in PBS film.
"He is my . . . as an artist": Vaill, p. 201.
"I have never . . . with Violette": Peter Martins speaking in PBS film.
"Maybe there was . . . more of an aura": Jowitt, p. 397.
"I just love . . . in the movies": Jowitt, p. 197.
"Balanchine wants . . . else has it": Jowitt, p. 198.
"I think you stink . . . Love, Tan": Jowitt, p. 199.
"plastered all over": Vaill, p. 209.
"I hated . . . Anxiety": Vaill, p. 210.
"Bette Davis . . . on a comb": Vaill, p. 212.
"The master . . . could you want?": PBS film.
"I don't mind . . . treated alphabetically": Vaill, p. 405.
"A lot of people . . . too complicated": Mark Morris in conversation with the author, New York, May 27, 2016. [Hereafter cited as Morris interview.]
"ninety minutes at hard labor": Arlene Croce, *Afterimages.* New York: Knopf, 1977, p. 404. [Hereafter cited as *Afterimages.*]
"If it really . . . tired or afraid": Vaill, p. 427.
"much anxiety . . . great anxiety about it": Vaill, p. 425.
"We all . . . Gogol's overcoat": Many sources, including Wikipedia, Jhumpa Lahiri's novel *The Namesake,* and others, but all are based on hearsay.
"He made this . . . learned from him": Mikhail Baryshnikov speaking in PBS film.

The Cage

"Can you imagine . . . *imagine?!*" Vaill, p. 417.

"a shocking . . . was queer . . . too late": Vaill, pp. 35, 36.

"first fuck": Jowitt, p. 80.

"time of being ousted by family": Vaill, p. 114.

"H.F.": Vaill, p. 75.

"He was . . . look at him": Vaill, p. 139.

"Nora is staying . . . feels like home": Jowitt, p. 178.

"And I said . . . wonderful time": Jowitt, p. 192.

"And then I read . . . like a dream": PBS film.

"decadent . . . procreation . . . you don't . . . nasty women": Jowitt, pp. 189, 190.

"literally . . . in offices": Vaill, p. 190.

"is actually . . . very thrown . . . no part of me": Vaill, p. 191.

"I don't see . . . fine the way it is": Jowitt, p. 190.

"I couldn't . . . won out": Vaill, p. 463.

"Can't you just . . . still dazed": Jowitt, p. 193.

"I've got to . . . see that": Jowitt, p. 51.

"I straighten . . . rules me v/much": Jowitt, p. 417.

"If my mother . . . not in": Vaill, p. 527.

"Mama Mama . . . and left": Vaill, p. 10.

Afternoon of a Faun

"*Afternoon* . . . obviousness of it . . . aura about her": *Afternoon of a Faun: Tanaquil Le Clercq*, a 2013 documentary film written and directed by Nancy Buirski. [Hereafter cited as *Afternoon* film.]

"Tanny Le Clercq . . . with that company!": Vaill, p. 154.

"All the ballets . . . for Tanny": *Afternoon* film.

"Balanchine . . . had a dialogue": Barbara Horgan speaking in *Afternoon* film.

"Dearest Tanny . . . like you do": *Afternoon* film.

"So many . . . looking at them too": Vaill, p. 200.

"Tanny . . . acuteness . . . I hope . . . Love, Tanny": *Afternoon* film.

"George is . . . be like him": Vaill, p. 201.

"Balanchine needed . . . work": Jacques D'Amboise speaking in *Afternoon* film.
"the dunes . . . very easily . . . Darling . . . All my love—T": Vaill, pp. 264, 265.
"By the time . . . come back": Jacques D'Amboise speaking in *Afternoon* film.
"Be of good . . . Dear Jerry . . . I cried": Vaill, p. 268.
"I keep asking . . . balance on its tail . . . with some people": *Afternoon* film.
"It's almost . . . has it . . . Dearest Jerry . . . dream them": *Afternoon* film.
"Balanchine never . . . the one": Barbara Horgan speaking in *Afternoon* film.
"My two . . . of Tanny's": Arthur Mitchell speaking in *Afternoon* film.
"She was . . . live alone": Randy Bourscheidt speaking in *Afternoon* film.
"It's one . . . starting to diminish": *Afternoon* film.
"Tanny's . . . in her life": Barbara Horgan speaking in *Afternoon* film.
"I love you . . . I love you": *Afternoon* film.
"Isn't it . . . for dancing": Vaill, p. 463.
"Jerry . . . it was home": Vaill, p. 521.

West Side Story

"Jerry R. called . . . for the book": Vaill, p. 250.
"I didn't like . . . popular theater?": PBS film.
"I hear rhythms . . . feel the form": Vaill, p. 252
"a find": Vaill, p. 257.
"Jerry is the only . . . worth it": Stephen Sondheim speaking in PBS film.
"Chita . . . be a person": Chita Rivera speaking in PBS film.
"You're way . . . forget Anita": Jowitt, p. 270.
"Jerry and Lenny had argued . . . in front of Lenny": Shawn, p. 146.
"Take that Hollywood shit out!": Vaill, p. 287.

"really shocking . . . left the theater": Shawn, p. 146.

"any and all rights . . . suggested by me": Jowitt, p. 274.

"I know . . . the way I am": Shawn, p. 145.

"I thought . . . more robustly": PBS film.

"I like *Peter Pan* . . . terribly moving": Morris interview.

"dwindle from . . . monsters": George Orwell, "Charles Dickens," in *The Collected Essays, Journalism and Letters of George Orwell.* New York: Harcourt Brace Jovanovich, 1968, Volume I, p. 424.

"the cast were . . . phony Puerto Rican": Morris interview.

"They do dances . . . rest of the dance": Jowitt, p. 275.

"The first time . . . I tell you . . . agony": Vaill, pp. 286, 287.

"one of the greatest . . . 'Cool' . . . I want you to meet . . . genius and director": Videorecording of "Cool" as presented on the *Ed Sullivan Show*, September 14, 1958; Jerome Robbins Dance Division, New York Public Library, call number MGZIA 4-6198 JRC.

"I'd like . . . Thank you": Videorecording of Academy Awards, 1962; Jerome Robbins Dance Division, New York Public Library, call number MGZIA 4-6199 JRC.

Fiddler on the Roof

"They told me . . . moment there": Jowitt, p. 11, and Vaill, p. 16.

"Sonia and Mother . . . thunderbolts . . . inflexions, songs": Jowitt, pp. 9, 10, 11.

"develop right . . . still alive . . . and rejected": Vaill, p. 197.

"One day . . . out of that": Vaill, p. 318.

"run-of-the-mill musical . . . I'M GOING . . . EXCITED": Vaill, p. 361.

"What's the show *about?*": Jowitt, p. 353.

"Dear Zee . . . Please": Jowitt, p. 355.

"lacklustre . . . pedestrian": Jowitt, p. 356.

"Jerry, what . . . things a day": Vaill, p. 369.

"Any man . . . I forgive everything": Vaill, p. 371.

"and threw . . . know all that": Vaill, p. 373.

"I think . . . Herald Square": Vaill, p. 373.

"the most . . . ever made": Pauline Kael, "A Bagel with a Bite Out of It," *The New Yorker,* November 13, 1971.

"explosive . . . primitive beast?": Shawn, p. 223.

"What was normal . . . The rights and duties . . . Freud was . . . neuroses": John Murray Cuddihy, *The Ordeal of Civility.* New York: Basic Books, 1974, pp. 64, 36–37, 89.

"Cuddihy is . . . deception": Hugh Lincoln, "Id of the Yid," accessible online at http://library.flawlesslogic.com/yid.htm.

"I affect . . . Jew self": Vaill, pp. 456, 457.

Dances at a Gathering

"she took . . . work with her": Bernier interview.

"It's a little . . . in the music": Jowitt, p. 366.

"In an empty studio . . . which is satisfying": Bernier interview.

"the fabulous . . . that one": Morris interview.

"More, more . . . keep eating!": Vaill, p. 411.

"*Dances at* . . . anyone else": Morris interview.

"He was drawn . . . are you looking?": Emily Coates in conversation with the author, New York, November 15, 2016. [Hereafter cited as Coates interview.]

"but the way . . . forward or backward": Bernier interview.

"Did DaaG . . . Sterns et al.": Jowitt, p. 388.

"Hesperian fables . . . here only": John Milton, *Paradise Lost and Selected Poetry and Prose.* New York: Holt, Rinehart and Winston, 1951, p. 86 (Book IV, lines 250–51).

"Jerry always . . . Forty-Second Street": Vaill, p. 293.

"and gave . . . no other comment . . . so transparent . . . is about": Vaill, p. 412.

"the great hit . . . in the fifties": *Afterimages*, pp. 285–6.

The Goldberg Variations

"It was like . . . start over . . . to the beginning": Vaill, pp. 419, 420.

"Mostly I feel . . . *Goldberg Variations*": Bernier interview.

"I'd give . . . tremendous": Jowitt, p. 107.

"A special feature . . . even most adults": Jowitt, p. 4.

"And he was late . . . to counts . . . The perimeter . . . you want": Bernier interview.

"very big and architectural": Jowitt, p. 392.

"They're depending . . . And then I hear . . . dancer to life": Brief videotape about *The Goldberg Variations* originally made for the New York City Ballet website (accessible at https://www.you tube.com/watch?v=yZVIKIhrAGw).

"terrible . . . DEPRESSION": Vaill, p. 416.

"Goldberg is ninety . . . puts me to sleep": *Afterimages*, pp. 404–5.

"I am more . . . communicative gesture": Jowitt, p. 395.

"the last new creation . . . important to him . . . cartwheel on the right . . . A score like . . . malleable in his hands": Coates interview.

"When he saw . . . equals with him": Coates interview.

"Misha, if it's . . . It's a keeper": Rehearsal tapes of *Suite of Dances* preserved at the Jerome Robbins Dance Division, New York Public Library, call numbers MGZIDF 535, MGZIDF 372, and MGZIA 4-6001 JRC.

In Memory Of . . .

"Whenever we did . . . ten and twelve": Bernier interview.

"It's left . . . the galaxy": Jowitt, p. 458.

"ballet-masters": Jowitt, p. 461.

"Gee, I'd like . . . to life again": Bernier interview.

"I started the ballet . . . those statues . . . That's why . . . can give you . . . When I found . . . many years later": Bernier interview.

"should not be connected . . . peace for themselves": Bernier interview.

"I'd gotten . . . Death figure . . . We all fused . . . performance of it": Bernier interview.

"It was hard . . . on himself": Jowitt, p. 475.

"I felt a big . . . dropped away": Vaill, p. 516.

"I can't show . . . all the time": Vaill, p. 509.

"He had a stroke . . . of his life . . . When he . . . human man": Coates interview.

"Goodbye . . . bless you too": Vaill, p. 527.

Coda

"You know, Violette . . . preconception": Jowitt, p. 412.

"You know, dear . . . he's *good*": Jowitt, p. 411.

"Looking at Chris Wheeldon's . . . echo of Jerry": Coates interview.

"Robbins wasn't . . . is unapproachable": Morris interview.

"Well, our big rumble . . . I love that": Morris interview.

"He's an inspiration . . . I miss him": Mikhail Baryshnikov speaking in PBS film.

"Because there's no way . . . statements about them": Bernier interview.

ACKNOWLEDGMENTS

My largest debt, as always in a project like this, is to those whose research precedes and underlies mine. Deborah Jowitt and Amanda Vaill, in their respective masterful biographies *Jerome Robbins: His Life, His Theater, His Dance* (2004) and *Somewhere: The Life of Jerome Robbins* (2006), both did full justice to the man who is our joint subject. Still, I am grateful to Yale's Jewish Lives series for deciding that yet another Robbins biography was necessary, giving me a chance to explore the work of a master I had never fully appreciated until now.

That exploration was made possible not only by the incomparable Jerome Robbins Dance Division of the New York Public Library, but also by the dance companies—the San Francisco Ballet, the American Ballet Theatre, and above all the New York City Ballet—which generously gave me press seats so I could witness live performances of Robbins's work. I was also greatly assisted by a semester-long fellowship at New York University's Center for Ballet and the Arts in the fall of 2016. The CBA's guiding spirit, Jennifer Homans, shared with me some of her bountiful knowledge about all things balletic and Balanchinian, and enabled me to meet up with Emily Coates and Amanda Vaill, both of whom gave me essential help on this book. Other CBA fellows, including Pam Tanowitz, John Heginbotham, Dana Mills, Meryl Rosofsky, and Tarik O'Regan, provided welcome stimulation and suggestive ideas over the course of our semester together.

Among those who deserve my special thanks are Mark Morris, who allowed himself to be interviewed in depth on the subject of Jerome Robbins and his influence on dance; Marina Harss, who conveyed some of Alexei Ratmansky's thoughts about Robbins to me; Ara Guzelimian, who first alerted me to the film *Afternoon of a Faun;* Milina Barry, who sent me the link to the New York City Ballet's informative *Goldberg Variations* video; Ben Taylor, who knew Jerry Robbins personally and was able to confirm my take on him; Allen Shawn, whose biography of Leonard Bernstein (also part of the Jewish Lives series) proved invaluable in my research; and John Branch, who transcended his role as proofreader, becoming both fact-checker and sounding-board. My good friend Arthur Lubow, always a source of sustenance and commiseration when I am writing, is especially useful when it comes to biographical projects, since he is an eminent biographer himself; so are my friends Brenda Wineapple, Mark Stevens, Annalyn Swan, and Jean Strouse. I owe thanks to all five of them for their conversational help, as well as to my husband, Richard Rizzo, whose lifelong interest in dance has supported and enhanced my own.

Finally, I once again need to thank Ileene Smith, my treasured editor on this and three previous books. She not only came up with the Jerome Robbins assignment in the first place; she also performed her usual editorial miracles on the manuscript, stood by me at every turn of events, and made the whole publishing process seem like a congenial, intimate enterprise. Hers is a rare gift, and I am grateful to be its beneficiary.

INDEX

continued on next page